The Negotiation Edge

The Negotiation Edge

Compete | Collaborate | Compromise

Lessons learned from 25 of my best and worst negotiations versus big retail, professional sports leagues, streaming platforms, TV cable networks, Hollywood studios, and celebrities.

Mike Saksa

Billion-dollar entertainment, sports, and retail negotiator

BEP

BUSINESS EXPERT PRESS

Leader in applied, concise business books

The Negotiation Edge: Compete | Collaborate | Compromise

Copyright © Business Expert Press, LLC, 2024

Cover design by Charlene Kronstedt

Interior design by Exeter Premedia Services Private Ltd., Chennai, India

First published in 2024 by
Business Expert Press, LLC
222 East 46th Street, New York, NY 10017
www.businessexpertpress.com

ISBN-13: 978-1-63742-571-8 (paperback)
ISBN-13: 978-1-63742-572-5 (e-book)

Business Expert Press Human Resource Management and
Organizational Behavior Collection

First edition: 2024

10 9 8 7 6 5 4 3 2 1

Description

The Negotiation Edge is a two-part book that will make you a better negotiator.

The first half is a negotiating tutorial complete with checklists and worksheets. It details on how to engage, prepare, select a leader, build a support team, identify roles, set communication guidelines, instruct meeting behavior, read the other side, and determine the best strategies (compete | collaborate | compromise) using a three-act negotiating structure.

The second half of the book is the author's 25 best and worst negotiating experiences with his insightful lessons learned with Wal-Mart, Amazon, Target, NFL, NBA, NHL, PBS, National Geographic, BBC, Netflix, Warner Bros., Disney, Universal, Fox, Paramount, Sony, Lionsgate, Tiger Woods, Oprah Winfrey, and Martha Stewart.

Keywords

improve negotiating skills; crisis management how to survive, adapt, and thrive; business disruption; negotiation case studies and experiences; business and film school; top negotiator for retail industry

Contents

Foreword

How Did This Happen?

My negotiating journey started early in my career with three catastrophic business events: The Tylenol poisonings, RJR Nabisco leveraged buyout (*Barbarians at the Gate*), and the AOL–Time Warner merger. In these situations, I was a middle-management stakeholder observing my fate being negotiated by the top executives at my companies. These were great learning experiences and life-changing events. I learned how to *survive* each difficult environment, *adapt* to a new work culture, and then *thrive* with new skills under the new management direction.

Rising from the dumpster fire of the AOLTW merger, I was trained to lead negotiations from both sides of the table: *acquiring* content for Warner Bros. Home Entertainment and *selling/licensing* content to retailers and streaming platforms. After 20 years with Warner Bros., I was hired by Redbox to negotiate content deals with movie studios, independent producers, and video game companies. My unique perspectives from each side of the negotiating table are in this book.

Rarely does one enter a negotiation without support from supervisors, colleagues, and staff. Throughout this book, I use the term *we* to indicate my negotiations were a group effort. My successes have been paved by Dave Chester, Tylenol Regional Sales Manager, Norm Vergara Nabisco Group Product Manager, Jim Cardwell, Warner Bros. President and Mark Horak, Warner Bros. and Redbox President.

The people across the table force you to be a better negotiator, so I am grateful to all the content owners, producers, agents, buyers, and executives at Wal-Mart, Target, Amazon, Netflix, Apple, Comcast, NFL, NBA, NHL, WCW, National Geographic, PBS, BBC, Warner Bros., Disney, Fox, Universal, Paramount, Sony, Lionsgate, Harpo Productions, MSLO Productions, Dualstar, Microsoft, Activision, Ubisoft, and Ingram. And finally, I appreciate my colleagues and staff members at Warner Bros. and Redbox, who rode the roller coaster of negotiations with me, providing both informational and emotional support.

Introduction

Improve Your Career With Better Negotiating Skills

The objective of this book is to learn how to gain the negotiation edge through superior preparation and effectively using compete, collaborate, and compromise strategies. Although every negotiation is different, using this method will improve your results and advance your career.

Many believe that successful negotiating only requires rational thinking and a sense of fairness. This overly simplistic approach often leads to disappointing results. You tend to settle for less, blaming the difficult circumstances or the other side's unyielding behavior. The only performance feedback is your self-review with the "I should have said this or done that" critique. You move on to the next negotiation believing it will be different, but your lack of skills and knowledge generate the same suboptimal results. You are stuck in the NDR cycle: Negotiate–Disappointment–Repeat.

Learning negotiation skills will improve your career in many ways. The primary benefit is with your immediate job responsibilities. Negotiation skills improve performance with external business partners and vendors. A secondary benefit is with career opportunities such as job interviews, promotions, raises, and job exits. Knowing how to effectively negotiate creates better jobs, higher compensation, and appropriate separation packages. Another benefit is having more productive relationships with supervisors, colleagues, and staff members. Knowing how to negotiate your needs and wants to the mutual benefit of others will make you a valued employee and raise your profile in the company.

The focus of this book is improving business transaction negotiations with outside partners and vendors, given that transactions are the engine of commerce. The first half instructs how to gain the negotiation edge by improving your execution of engagement, leadership, team building, behavior, preparation, reading the other side, strategies, and the three acts of a negotiation. During each of these phases, you will learn how and when to use the three key strategies: compete, collaborate, and compromise. The bonus chapter, Content Agreements, instructs how to negotiate for qualitative assets such as entertainment content or intellectual property.

The second half of the book details the lessons learned from my best and worst 25 negotiations. The breadth and depth of this learning will guide you in whichever situation or career path you choose. These entertaining case studies provide deeper insights from my experiences with a wide variety of leaders, companies, and industries:

- **Companies in Crisis**: Tylenol, Nabisco, and AOL–Time Warner
- **Big Retail**: Amazon, Wal-Mart, and Target Department Stores
- **Professional Sports Leagues**: The NFL, NBA, NHL, and WCW
- **Television Companies**: National Geographic, PBS, and the BBC
- **Celebrities**: Tiger Woods, Oprah Winfrey, Martha Stewart, and the Olsen Twins
- **Disruptors**: Netflix and Redbox
- **Movie Studios**: Warner Bros., Fox, Universal, Disney, Paramount, Sony, and Lionsgate

PART ONE

How to Gain and Leverage the Edge

This section provides a comprehensive instruction "how-to" negotiate from the negotiation proposal to the final performance review. This practical guide includes worksheets and checklists to use with future negotiations.

CHAPTER 1

The Negotiation Engagement

How to Gain the Opening Edge

Starting a Negotiation

A negotiation ensues when one party believes that a transaction with a second party has the potential to create mutual benefits. The process starts when one side reaches out to the other with a conversation and a document to determine the level of interest. This can be a *letter of intent* (LOI) or a *memorandum of understanding* (MOU). These documents contain detailed descriptions of the main terms with no vagueness or ambiguity in the wording. The main terms are called the *pillars of the agreement*:

- Product or service
- Length of agreement
- Geography
- Payment terms

A good business practice is having two other types of agreements signed before sending or receiving the LOI or MOU. The first is an *exclusive negotiation agreement* (ENA), which contractually sets a period of time when no other entity can negotiate for the same assets. The second, *nondisclosure agreement* (NDA), is a contract to ensure all aspects of the proposal and subsequent negotiation are confidential. All of the aforementioned documents should be sent electronically with encryption to a secured platform to avoid unauthorized reading or copying.

Once you receive an LOI, the first step is to define your *overall goal* and develop the *negotiation objective*. The first is qualitative, and the latter is quantitative. The goal and objective may appear similar and are often loosely interchanged; however, each has a specific meaning and usefulness to the negotiation process.

Define the Overall Goal of the Negotiation

The overall goal of the negotiation is the *qualitative value* of the negotiation. It is how your company wants to be perceived internally by management, employees, and stakeholders and externally by customers and industry. The goal needs to be consistent with company values or mission statement.

The next step is to estimate the qualitative impact of the proposed negotiation. The potential upside of a successful negotiation can be an improved market standing and an enhanced company image. Next, determine the qualitative impact should the negotiation fail to produce an agreement. The most common downsides are tarnished executive reputation, wasted resources, distracted employees, or a lower industry standing. There can be an upside in a failed negotiation such as better understanding of your market position or a forced change in strategic direction.

The next step is to determine the impact of *not engaging* in a negotiation. The downside can be the regret of a missed opportunity. The upside is not having to commit resources to a situation with a low probability of a positive outcome. Not engaging in a difficult negotiation saves not only time and money but reputation as well.

The following chart (Figure 1.1) will aid you in determining the proposal's net impact on your overall goal. First, write the overall goal of the negotiation. Then, in each of the three scenarios, detail the upsides and downsides in qualitative terms. The last row *Net Result* will answer whether this negotiation will get you to where you want to be as a company.

Overall Goal of the Negotiation:		
Negotiation Outcome	What are the Positive Impacts	What are the Negative Impacts
1. Engaged and reached an agreement.		
2. Engaged and failed to reach an agreement.		
3. Decline to engage in the negotiation.		
Net Result:	Rationale:	

Figure 1.1 Overall goal of the negotiation chart

Set the Negotiation Objective

The negotiation objective is the *quantitative value* of the agreement. It is singular in nature, measurable, and set within a specific time period. It must be able to answer *yes or no* to the question, "Did the negotiation achieve the objective?" The objective is a financial metric such as profit or an aggregation of multiple business targets. The objective must consider the limits of resources, scale, and time. The more focused the objective, the higher the probability of attaining it.

The length of the negotiation process will have an influence on the ability to achieve the objective. The longer the negotiation, the greater the potential for market fluctuations to impact the objective. If the process is drawn out, the proposal needs updates to reset the probability of achieving the objective. Financial software makes this task easier to perform.

Internal and external pressures should be avoided to adjust the objective unnecessarily as the process unfolds. Loosely defined targets, such as *synergistic savings,* tend to be difficult to measure and are often overstated late in the negotiation. *Market share* is another dangerous negotiation objective as attempting to acquire scale often leads to overpaying and creates cashflow problems.

Long negotiations have an emotional impact. If you find yourself thinking, "we've come too far" or "have worked too long" not to do this deal, then stop and reevaluate the terms. Bad deals get made when one side loses sight of the measurable objective and only supports the deal with qualitative terms like image or perception in the market. Justifying a deal that has become riskier is a dangerous behavior and can result in the *winner's curse*—a completed agreement generating bad results.

An overlooked part of setting the objective is estimating the hard and soft costs required to perform the negotiation. Hard costs are easy to measure in currency and can be estimated by accountants, attorneys, and consultants. A common cost is the deposit or escrow payment required to ensure one side is committed to seeing the negotiation to deal completion. Soft costs are disruption to your organization's ongoing operations and are more difficult to measure. The time commitment of the negotiating team, employee distractions, and the impact on company morale are common negotiation soft costs. To better manage the hard and soft cost parts of the process, consider hiring outside specialists to provide an objective perspective with minimal internal influences or disruptions.

The final step is determining the probability for success. Management support, adequate time, and resources along with favorable market conditions are key factors. Setting the probability of success indirectly reflects the level of risk your organization will accept to move forward with the negotiation. The following chart (Figure 1.2) guides you in defining the negotiation objective for the proposal.

The Negotiation Objective Summary	
Categories	**Key Metrics**
Negotiation Objective	
Time Period	
Internal Resources Required	
Hard Costs	
Soft Costs	
External Market Assumptions	
Probability of Success	

Figure 1.2 The negotiation objective summary chart

Identify the Key Components

The scale and complexity of an upcoming negotiation can be overwhelming. The amount of information can both guide and confuse you. To help you get organized, categorize all the preliminary information into five key components. Although all negotiations are different, the components are the same.

The Negotiation Deadline

Deadlines drive negotiations to a conclusion. Time creates pressure to make progress or end the process. The best situation is when both sides have the same deadline. Highly collaborative, multiple-party negotiations have a critical need for a common deadline. One party gains the edge when the other side has greater need for a shorter or firmer deadline. On a positive note, leaders tend to be more open to compromise as a deadline approaches.

There are methods to minimize an edge leading up to an unfavorable deadline. One party can protect themselves with an *out clause*, which allows the party to abandon the agreement based on predetermined and mutually approved conditions or operational metrics. These clauses, known as *schmuck insurance,* can overcomplicate a deal and be hard to negotiate. Another one is to have a *contingency clause* forcing one side to pay a fee if a deal is not completed at the deadline. Another option for ongoing relationships is to have *automatic extensions* to minimize the potential for business disruption.

There are two methods to preemptively force progress with firm deadlines. The first is to have *right of first refusal* where one party must offer the other party their initial deal proposal. This allows the other side to react to a new deal before any other party sees it. The other variation is offering the *right of last refusal* when one of the parties wants better terms and is allowed to negotiate with other entities. If a viable offer is presented by a third party, the new deal terms must be offered to the current partner to match it.

The Stakeholders of the Negotiation

Stakeholders can influence the outcome of the negotiation. Getting their support increases the probability of a successful negotiation. Conversely, having dissatisfied stakeholders can derail a negotiation. Stakeholders can play it both ways by assigning blame for *failing* to complete a *good* agreement or *successfully* completing a *bad* agreement. They can be a difficult group to manage due to their unyielding self-interests. Do not allow them to directly participate in the negotiations or have contact with the other side.

The variety of stakeholders adds complexity to the negotiation as internal and external interests are often in conflict. Being collaborative with stakeholders is time-consuming and can be a threat to the confidentiality of the negotiation. It is best for leaders to give information early on a *need-to-know* basis and be selective beyond that. Establish the impression you are collaborating by listening to their needs and giving strong intentions to negotiate on their behalf. If they sense you are not, they will try to get a seat at the negotiating table and can be very disruptive to the proceedings. Be careful, they can undermine your success even if they are not in the room.

In Figure 1.3, make a list of the stakeholders and rank their order from most influential to least influential. Then identify their needs and wants in the negotiation. *Needs* are the highest priorities and must-haves, and *wants* are lower priorities and like-to-haves. Then assign a value such as an expected revenue enhancement or cost savings. Take this a step further by assigning the probability of getting the other side to agree to each of your stakeholder's needs and wants.

Stakeholder Profile Needs and Wants Summary			
Stakeholder Rank of Influence	Stakeholder Priorities	Estimated Value	Probability of Getting
Name #1	Needs:		
	Wants:		
Name #2	Needs:		
	Wants:		
Name #3	Needs:		
	Wants:		
Total Stakeholder Value			

Figure 1.3 Stakeholder needs and wants summary chart

Profile the Other Side

A negotiation is the formal courtship of a business relationship. While it helps to personally like the people on the other side, mutual respect is more important. The foundation of a productive working relationship is based on two key traits: *integrity* and *trust*. The probability of having a successful negotiation starts with *understanding the motivations* of the other side and your *ability to work with them.*

The following competitive profile chart (Figure 1.4) will help determine how the two organizations compare to each other. The profile includes the key factors: *the negotiation leader, strengths, vulnerabilities, appetite for risk, integrity/trust,* and *their urgency to complete an agreement.* These organizational traits are listed on the far left (yours) and far right (theirs) columns. Each trait is ranked on a scale of 1 being low and 5 being high. The two scores are compared by subtracting your score from their score to create a gap score. The smaller the differences, the higher the probability of reaching an agreement. Large differences will indicate where there is a negotiation edge.

The following example indicates an even match of key traits between the organizations and fewer opportunities to establish a negotiation edge.

Competitive Profile Key Traits Comparison (Example)				
Your Key Traits	Your Score (1–5)	Negotiation Gap Score	Their Score (1–5)	Their Key Traits
Leadership	5	1	4	Leadership
Strengths	4	(1)	5	Strengths
Vulnerabilities	3	0	3	Vulnerabilities
Risk Comfort Level	1	(2)	3	Risk Comfort Level
Integrity/Trust Factor	5	2	3	Integrity/Trust Factor
Urgency for the Deal	3	(1)	4	Urgency for the Deal
Subtotal	21	(1)	22	Subtotal

Figure 1.4 Competitive profile key traits comparison chart example

Market Conditions

External conditions can change the value of the proposed agreement over the course of the negotiating narrative. You need to monitor and adjust to a fluctuating marketplace. Do the market analysis prior to starting the negotiation to be comfortable with the anticipated level of volatility risk. Do not sign an agreement when you know a fluctuating market makes the probability for achieving the objective lower than when you started.

If outside conditions can make the deal terms unfavorable, attempt to include adjustment clauses.

Negotiation Initiation Decision

Now that you have analyzed your side, their side, and the market conditions, it is time to make the decision whether you should engage in a negotiation. The leader and approver of the deal should collaborate completing the following chart (Figure 1.5):

- Do you believe both the goal and the objective are achievable? Rate your confidence on a scale of 1 being low and 10 being high in the far right column.
- Are the pillars of the agreement (product, length of agreement, geography, and cost) favorable to you. Rate your confidence level on the scale of 1 to 10 in the far right column.
- Do you have an edge in any of the key components? (deadline, stakeholders, other side's motivation, and market conditions) Rate your confidence 1 to 10 in the far right column.

Once you have completed the assessments of the goals, objective, pillars, and key components, total the *Initiation Decision Score* column. The total score will guide your decision and provide an early indication which of the three negotiation strategies may work best: compete, collaborate, or compromise.

Negotiation Initiation Scorecard or Recommended Strategy

- Strong: 80–100—Compete Strategy
- Good: 50–79—Collaborate Strategy
- Weak: 40–49—Compromise Strategy
- Less than 39—Do Not Engage

Negotiation Initiation Decision		
Key Factors	Description/ Explanation	Initiation Decision Score (1 low to 10 high)
1. Negotiation Goal		Achievable #
2. Negotiation Objective		Achievable #
3. Product or Service		Favorable #
4. Length of Agreement		Favorable #
5. Geography/Territory		Favorable #
6. Cost/Payment Terms		Favorable #
7. Negotiation Deadline		Advantage #
8. Stakeholders Profile		Advantage #
9. Other Side's Profile		Advantage #
10. Market Conditions		Advantage #
Recommendation to Engage in a Negotiation: GO or NO GO?	Rationale:	Total Score:

Figure 1.5 Negotiation initiation decision chart

Negotiation Engagement Decision: Checklist

Internal Review

- ❏ Does the negotiation fit your company goal?
- ❏ Does the negotiation have a measurable objective?
- ❏ What is the probability of achieving the goal and objective?
- ❏ Who will lead the negotiation?
- ❏ Does the leader have a reliable negotiation team?
- ❏ Who has authority to approve the negotiation?
- ❏ Who are the internal stakeholders?
- ❏ Does your organization have sufficient resources for a negotiation?
- ❏ Does management support the negotiation?
- ❏ How will the negotiation process affect your employees?

External Review

- ❏ Who are the external stakeholders?
- ❏ How many parties in the deal?
- ❏ Who is the other side's leader and approver?
- ❏ What are their needs and wants?
- ❏ What are their strengths and vulnerabilities?
- ❏ Which side wants the deal more?
- ❏ What is the expected tone of the negotiation?
- ❏ Can you work with the other side?
- ❏ How stable are the market conditions?
- ❏ Who will be critiquing the negotiations?

The Deal Structure

- ❏ Does the LOI include the pillars of the agreement: product, length of term, geography, and payment terms?
- ❏ What is the deal's worth?
- ❏ How complex is the deal: number of terms and its relative volatility?
- ❏ Are you comfortable with the estimated level of risk?
- ❏ Have you protected your downside?
- ❏ How much will you benefit in the upside?
- ❏ Does the length of the deal term have upside or risk?

CHAPTER 2

Negotiation Leaders

Effective Traits and Behaviors

Appointing the Negotiation Leader

Top management will appoint a negotiation leader *before deciding* how to respond to a negotiation proposal. The appointed leader will have primary responsibility for the outcome of the negotiation. Leaders have earned this assignment by demonstrating their knowledge, judgment, and ability to represent the company. Their selection gives the company the best chance to succeed.

It is important for both sides to clearly define who has authority to *negotiate* and *approve* terms of the agreement and the total agreement prior to entering a negotiation. A layer of complexity is added when the negotiation leader has limited approval authority. However, there are multiple benefits to organizations to separate the responsibilities. First, the approver not being in the meetings is insulated from the emotional influences of the negotiation. Second, the less experienced leader is protected from having to make quick decisions and potential mistakes. Third, the delayed communication between the leader and the approver provides more time to analyze proposals and develop an optimal response.

Another advantage separating the two responsibilities is when the negotiation leader plays good cop by giving the impression to be working with the other side against their own approver, the *bad cop*. The good cop/bad cop advantage lasts a relatively shorter time. Eventually, the other side will get frustrated for not having direct and timely feedback from the approver. Another point of frustration is the negotiator having contrarian points of view with the approver. It is important to give clear, consistent, and timely responses to the approving source. Anything less, the lead negotiator quickly loses credibility with the other side.

A leader's reputation and career can rise or fall inside and outside the company with one negotiation. The amount of scrutiny the leader receives increases proportionately to the size of the negotiation. The leader's standing will never be the same after an important negotiation.

Untrained and inexperienced leaders tend to avoid difficult negotiations for fear of failing and not being comfortable with confrontation. This type of leader will get a reputation of being overly cautious. By not engaging, a leader may miss opportunities for financial success and, at the very least, a chance to gather competitive intelligence and gain valuable experience. Conversely, some negotiation leaders believe they have a fiduciary responsibility to engage all opportunities, regardless of the downside potential.

Learning what it takes to be an effective negotiation leader will help your career. Learning the traits and behaviors of skilled negotiation leaders provides guidance for your career in these four areas:

- Gaining support from the management of your organization
- Preparing and managing your staff to high levels of productivity
- Becoming a valued colleague
- Improving your relationships with people outside of your organization

Ten Key Responsibilities of a Negotiation Leader

Experienced negotiation leaders have a keen understanding of their responsibilities. The 10 key responsibilities for leading a negotiation are as follows:

- Achieve the negotiation goal and objective
- Manage the entire negotiation process to its satisfactory conclusion
- Identify the negotiation type and successfully prepare for the negotiation
- Determine and execute the appropriate strategy
- Perform within the scope of authority and gain management approvals where necessary

- Build the negotiation team and maintain an appropriate level of confidentiality
- Identify key stakeholders and manage their engagement to a satisfactory level
- Develop and execute the engagement and communication plans
- Establish a productive relationship with the other side, regardless of the outcome
- Outsource a 360-degree performance review of the leader and negotiation team

Ten Personality Traits of a Successful Negotiation Leader

No two negotiation leaders are alike; however, the successful ones have recognizable personality traits that lead to success:

- Respected by the other side
- High emotional intelligence quotient
- Credibility
- Integrity and trustworthiness
- Confidence with humility
- Accurate self-awareness
- Positive attitude
- Patience
- Comfortable with performance risk
- Attention to detail

Ten Behaviors of a Successful Negotiation Leader

Negotiations have a lot of moving parts and require specific behaviors to navigate through the many peaks and valleys. Successful negotiation leaders have consistently demonstrated the following behaviors to deliver a satisfactory outcome:

- Believes an agreement is better for all parties
- Demonstrates assertiveness without putting the other side on the defensive

- Possesses excellent listening skills and doesn't dominate the discussion
- Communicates position without emotion and does not express frustration
- Discusses all topics with the appropriate level of detail
- Frames issues from the benefit of the other party
- Uses leverage only at the optimal time
- Does not *over-lawyer* the situation
- Knows the optimal timing to walk away from an unsatisfactory negotiation
- Uses superior debating skills

The Need for a Negotiation Consultant/Advisor/Coach

Depending on the organization's size and frequency of its negotiations, it may be best to outsource some or all of the negotiation's responsibilities. The time and expectations required to lead a negotiation can be overwhelming, especially if the leader has operating responsibilities. The leader's time commitment will increase if there is an organizational need for *stakeholder inclusivity* and *organizational transparency*. Companies in highly competitive, evolving industries with numerous vendors can benefit from either hiring consultants or training in-house executives.

It is rare to have a negotiation leader with all the skills necessary to complete a long and complex multiparty negotiation. When you need someone to climb a tree, sometimes it is better to hire an *outside* squirrel than to train the *in-house* turkey. If the leader has an obvious skill gap, it is beneficial to bring in someone to provide insights and guidance. It can be initiated by two sources: the *organization* asks the outsider to help the negotiation leader or *the leader* asks for help from a previous relationship.

Both the leader and consultant must have shared respect and trust between them based on the appreciation for each other's knowledge and experiences. The consultant or advisor cannot be a threat to the leader's standing in the organization. Both the leader and consultant need to know an unproductive working relationship will be transparent to the organization and likely tarnish both reputations.

An internal issue when hiring a negotiation consultant is the organization's other top executives may resent not having the opportunity to participate in a high-profile negotiation. This can cause resistance to supporting the consultant's work such as the ability to access critical information to prepare for the negotiation.

Consultant Capabilities

A trained negotiation consultant can deliver the following:

- Lead or advise the leader of a small internal negotiation team
- Gather input from all stakeholders
- Set realistic and objective performance metrics
- Ensure accuracy of projections by minimizing human error and bias
- Perform the necessary internal and external documentation
- Keep the negotiation moving forward
- Avoid miscommunication, human emotion, and personality conflicts
- Enhance confidentiality

Negotiation Leader Case Studies

Negotiation leaders have different personalities and processes to achieve success. The following are two case studies of leaders, one in entertainment and the other in sports, who have exceled in the art and science of negotiating.

Profile #1: Michael Eisner, Disney Ex-CEO

One of the most successful negotiators in the entertainment industry is Michael Eisner, the ex-CEO of Disney. Early in his career, he worked directly for the notoriously demanding Barry Diller, who earned his reputation as a tough negotiator. It was Eisner who took the art of negotiating to another level, but like the gunslingers of the Old West, his last big negotiation ended his career. The following is a summary of his biggest negotiations that established his reputation for good and eventually bad.

Negotiating for the Disney CEO Position

In 1984, Eisner was the president of Paramount Pictures working for studio chief Barry Diller. The studio was thriving with movie hits such as *48 Hours* and *Indiana Jones*, during which time Eisner was constantly networking to his advantage. Eisner befriended CAA superagent Michael Ovitz and industry reporter Tony Schwartz to subtly spread the word to the industry he was the driving force behind Paramount's success.

When the Disney board of directors expressed interest in hiring him as the CEO in 1984, Eisner displayed his negotiating savvy by courting the most influential board members, Stanley Gold and Roy Disney. After multiple formal interviews, Eisner thought he had the job and negotiated hard for 500k shares of Disney stock, which was significantly more than the previous CEO. Eisner may have negotiated too hard as the Disney board, led by Roy Disney, continued to look at other candidates.

When Paramount CEO Bludhorn died unexpectedly, Diller was passed over for the top spot and left to run Fox Studios. Eisner, sensing a negotiation edge with Disney, began negotiating with Western + Gulf CEO Martin Davis for the Paramount top job. He made a strategic negotiating error in telling Davis that he was about to get the Disney CEO position. Davis called his bluff. He fired Eisner and promoted Paramount's marketing head, Frank Mancuso. The firing increased the Disney board's uncertainty about Eisner. Now, he was unemployed and the Disney opportunity appeared to be fading away.

Eisner learned from his industry sources that the Disney board's other candidate was the highly respected business attorney Frank Wells. The board originally wanted a creative executive to run the company but was now leaning toward having a business executive. Frank Wells knew how to interact with board members and outside investors but did not have the creative experience.

Eisner knew Disney's ongoing failure at the box office increased their urgency for his creative skills. In a bold move, Eisner contacted Wells to convince him to be his right-hand man and go to the board as a packaged deal. Eisner was able to negotiate a $750k base salary, a $750k signing bonus, and 510k Disney shares and a 2 percent bonus for profits exceeding $100 million. Disney had never reached $100 million in profit, so it appeared to be a low risk sweetener by the board. In a matter of weeks, Eisner's negotiating skills enabled him to go from unemployed with an uncertain future to getting the highest paid studio job in Hollywood.

In four years, Disney would complete an amazing turnaround with an 80 percent increase in profitability. Eisner's fourth-year compensation included a bonus of $6.8 million and $33 million in exercised stock options, making him the highest paid executive in America.

Negotiating to Buy the ABC Network

Prior to 1993, television networks had to buy all their programing from external movie and television studios. That year, the FCC abolished the financial interest and syndication (Fin-Syn) regulation, allowing television networks to produce and distribute their own shows. This threatened a profitable revenue stream for studios like Disney, who made television programing for the networks. Without the fin-syn regulation, the movie studios wanted to vertically integrate by acquiring one of the three existing television networks: ABC, CBS, or NBC.

Eisner approached both CBS and Cap Cities in August 1995 at the Allen & Co. summit. At the time, CBS CEO Larry Tisch was in final negotiations to sell to Westinghouse. Tisch wanted to use Disney's interest in CBS to negotiate a higher price from Westinghouse. With the same competitive negotiation strategy, Eisner thought having a public meeting with Tisch at the Allen conference would motivate Cap Cities to sell to Disney.

Eisner first approached Warren Buffet, Cap Cities largest shareholder, to get his support. With Buffet's influence, Tom Murphy, CEO of Cap Cities gave Eisner a firm price: $19 billion in stock and cash. Eisner then used tactics that gave him his negotiation reputation. The first tactic was asking to get a little more to close the deal. Eisner wanted to show his board his dealmaker skills by getting a last-minute reduction in the deal price. Murphy was unmoved and stuck to his asking price.

Eisner's second negotiation tactic was using the phrase: *the employee you were negotiating with did not have the authority to make a deal.* Disney

CFO Tom Bollenbach was negotiating a much lower price with CBS. Eisner wanted a potential CBS verbal agreement as leverage to get Murphy to lower the ABC price. However; Tisch knew that if Eisner wasn't leading the negotiation, there was a low probability of getting a deal with Disney.

Eisner's third tactic is trying to get a long-term concession right before closing the deal. Again, Murphy resisted, and Eisner finally realized he wasn't going to get a better deal. He sensed Murphy's resolve and did not want to lose the deal because of his overnegotiating.

The Disney–ABC negotiation went from conversation to completion in two weeks. It was the second largest acquisition in U.S. history at the time. Eisner established his reputation as a visionary leader and tough negotiator.

Negotiating the Pixar Distribution Deal

The original Disney–Pixar distribution deal in 1994 was perhaps Eisner's greatest negotiation, but the deal eventually contributed to his downfall.

Disney began distributing Pixar movies with the release of *Toy Story* in 1995, the first film of a multipicture deal that was extremely favorable for Disney. Pixar would be responsible for all creative and pay Disney a marketing and distribution fee based on the film's revenue. The production costs and subsequent profits would be split 50/50. The key term of the deal was Disney ownership and control of the intellectual property for perpetuity across all media. Pixar's first film, *Toy Story* (1995), was a huge worldwide hit. The three properties in development *Bug's Life* (1998), *Toy Story 2* (1999), and *Monsters, Inc.* (2001) were looking to be hits as well. Jobs realized he made an error giving up control of the Pixar intellectual property rights in the deal.

By 2001, Pixar, now a popular movie brand, began negotiations for a new and better distribution deal with Disney. Jobs viewed himself as the *creative engine* behind Pixar and suggested to Eisner that he could manage Disney Animation as well. Jobs insisted on better terms such as paying a lower distribution fee, funding its own productions, keeping the profits, and retaining all the intellectual property rights retroactively with *Toy Story*, *Bug's Life*, and *Monsters Inc.* Retaining the rights to the original three movies was important to Jobs. Giving back a key deal point, especially control over highly valued assets, is something Eisner would not do. Both negotiation leaders had reached a very public impasse.

Eisner viewed Jobs as a *hired-hand* and believed he was more responsible for the success of Pixar. He was not going to materially change the deal terms, especially the copyright ownership. He used his relationships with the press to convey a superior position to Jobs. He attempted to frustrate and belittle Jobs to extend the current deal. Eisner made public disparaging comments such as "Negotiating with Jobs is like making an accord with a Shiite Muslim" and "Jobs created a computer or whatever he did, he was pretty good at it."

In 2004, Jobs announces to the industry he is seeking another distribution partner, as he could not work with Disney if Eisner was running the company. During talks with WB, he said "he would stay at Disney if he could throw pixie dust into the air and resolve his personal differences with Eisner."

While the public negotiations continued, the board was losing confidence in Eisner's leadership due to his other public feuds with Katzenberg and Ovitz. The board forced Eisner to resign under pressure in October 2004. Bob Iger became the CEO, and in 2006, he negotiated the acquisition of Pixar for $7.4 billion, making Jobs the largest Disney shareholder and giving him a seat on the board. Pixar's John Lassiter and Ed Catmull became coheads of a combined Pixar and Disney Animation division.

Lessons Learned From Michael Eisner Negotiations

- Gain support from current and future stakeholders before you need them.
- Create an edge by having alternative actions.
- When you recognize the other side is desperate, leverage the *big ask*.
- Leave something on the table, so the other side can save face.
- A negotiator's reputation is easy to form but difficult to change, so get it right early.

Profile #2: Jerry Jones, Owner of the Dallas Cowboys

In 1989, Jerry Jones, an Arkansas oil entrepreneur, was interested in buying the Dallas Cowboys.

The acquisition price was going to set a record for its time. Jones needed to know the future revenue potential to make the deal work financially. Jones had meetings with all the NFL vendors, including Dan Burke, the CEO of Cap Cities, owners of ESPN and ABC. The NFL television licensing revenue is shared equally by the 32 teams. Jones wanted to know how much the networks valued the league and the upside in future TV licensing.

Burke told Jones the networks needed the NFL to attract the highly desired 25- to 54-year-old male audience. He praised the efforts of then NFL commissioner, Pete Rozelle, for keeping the bidding process orderly for all three networks: NBC, ABC, and CBS. Rozelle made sure each network would get some programing at a fair price.

This is where Burke made a huge mistake. He expressed to Jones his concern for future negotiations if Rozelle was not the NFL's lead negotiator. An open uncontrolled process would create bidding wars, which the networks desperately wanted to avoid. Jones knew the benefits of highly competitive blind-bidding negotiations from the oil industry. The off-handed remark was just the kind of information Jones needed to hear.

Jones left the meeting confident the Cowboys $140 million acquisition price was a good value as he could extract significant upside in future TV license fees. The NFL's equitable process of the TV licensing negotiations was an opportunity for financial upside by going to a blind auction process. Jerry Jones' negotiation motto was "When the other side praises your lead negotiator, then you need to fire your negotiator."

Upon buying the Cowboys, Jones became the NFL owners' lead media negotiator. Jones disrupted the process by instituting a blind-bid auction for TV rights, which grew the average TV licensing revenue for each team from $32 million in 2011 to $200 million in 2021. The new deal negotiated in 2022 is a 10-year deal worth on average $312 million per team. Jerry Jones was inducted to the 2017 Pro Football Hall of Fame for generating unprecedented growth in TV licensing deals for the league and his fellow owners.

Lessons Learned From Jerry Jones Negotiation

- Negotiation edge is having superior knowledge of the deal's upside or downside.
- Gain competitive insights by *appearing to be* collaborative in social situations when opinions are less guarded.
- Negotiators need to be respected, but they do not have to be liked. Although being liked can help when the situation becomes tense and adversarial.

Negotiation Leadership: Key Traits and Behaviors Checklist

Successful Leader's Personality Traits

- ❑ Respected by the other side
- ❑ High emotional IQ
- ❑ Credibility
- ❑ Integrity and trustworthiness
- ❑ Confidence with humility
- ❑ Accurate self-awareness
- ❑ Positive attitude
- ❑ Patience
- ❑ Comfortable with performance risk
- ❑ Attention to detail

Successful Leader's Behaviors

- ❑ Believes an agreement is better for all parties
- ❑ Demonstrates assertiveness without putting the other side on the defensive
- ❑ Possesses excellent listening skills and doesn't dominate the discussion
- ❑ Communicates position without emotion and does not express frustration
- ❑ Discusses all topics with the appropriate level of detail
- ❑ Frames issues from the benefit of the other party
- ❑ Uses leverage only at the optimal time
- ❑ Does not *over-lawyer* the situation and uses superior debating skills
- ❑ Knows the optimal timing to walk away from an unsatisfactory negotiation

CHAPTER 3

Your Negotiation Team

How to Build and Manage It

One of the more challenging leadership responsibilities is building a dedicated team to assist the preparation and execution of the negotiation. A negotiation edge is created by assembling and managing a support team that is superior to the other side. A high-functioning team requires skills, work ethic, and personalities that fit specific roles. The selection is based on who *needs* to be on the team and not who *wants* to be. The team size and required skills are dependent on the negotiation's complexity and the number of influential stakeholders.

Negotiation Complexity

The complexity of a negotiation is a function of the number of proposed terms and expertise required to analyze, negotiate, and execute the agreement. Each team member has a specific role based on their skills, expertise, and ability to work with the leader and other team members. If the expertise is not available with internal candidates, it can be provided by outside specialists. Legal, banking, accounting, and tax consulting are commonly outsourced in negotiations.

The Number of Stakeholders

The number and variety of stakeholders will impact the size of the negotiating team. Providing analysis on terms impacting the stakeholders is a time-consuming responsibility. The leader can delegate for time efficiency by setting formal lines of communication between select staff members and stakeholders. The negotiating staff will ensure stakeholder's individual interests are being addressed in the preparatory meetings and keep them informed on an *as-needed basis* during the negotiations. Each staff member must respect the confidentiality of the negotiation and only communicate information that has been approved by the leader. Respect for the hierarchy and appreciation for confidentiality are valued traits for a negotiating team member.

The Core Negotiation Team

The core negotiation team consists of six people with specific skills and roles. The team size can expand with added complexities or be reduced when one person fills multiple roles. Some roles will be a priority over others depending on which discipline is more important to the negotiation.

The Team

- Negotiation Leader
- Strategy/analytics
- Development/ideas/solutions
- Notetaker/quantitative support/data source
- Liaison/qualitative support/responsible for executing the agreement
- Advisor/consultant (e.g., legal, finance, and tax)

The Selection Process

The negotiation leader will build a team that produces *effective teamwork, efficient communication,* and ensures *confidentiality.* Selecting members to be in the negotiating room is a difficult decision that requires thoughtfulness and sensitivity. Potential team members know having negotiation experience is good for professional development and careers. They want to be involved with a big negotiation with a high probability for success where they can claim their share of the responsibility for the outcome.

The potential for a failed negotiation will create the opposite condition. Potential team members will distance themselves from the negotiation leader. The aftermath of a failed negotiation creates a cultural depression similar to badly losing an athletic competition.

The negotiation support staff will feel entitled to attend for having participated in the prep work. They will be upset when not selected to be in the negotiation room. It is important for the leader to make them feel appreciated so that they stay loyal to the process. Staff resentment can create a confidentiality risk to the negotiation. Keep them informed on a *need-to-know* basis.

Sometimes an individual's reputation or behavior will keep them out of the negotiation room. The following should not be in the negotiation room:

Reputations

- Has a selfish motivation and a *what's in it for me* attitude
- Has a ridged, contrarian point of view that can undermine the agreement
- Lacks self-control
- Lacks the loyalty and trust to keep information confidential

Meeting Behaviors

- Repeats oneself or others' comments
- Circles back to previously agreed points
- Interrupts others often
- Hijacks discussion topics
- Extends discussions to irrelevant topics
- Pontificates trying to prove his/her intelligence and knowledge

Team Roles and Positions

Negotiation Leader (NL): NL sits in the middle of the table across from the other side's leader and controls the discussion. The leader is the only one permitted to speak to the other side but may direct a team member to communicate a fact to support a point or invalidate the other side's position. The prepared leader sticks to the scripted talking points and focuses on the other leader's content, tone, and body language.

Strategist—Right Position 1 (RP1): RP1 sits to the immediate right of the NL in a key *defensive* position. RP1 takes notes on the other side's talking points to adjust strategies for subsequent meetings. Provides analysis and information to support the leader's position or discredit the other side. Communication to leader is subtle, timely, and 100 percent accurate. RP1 provides only the necessary details as too many can interfere with NL's thought process. Comes prepared with relevant support documents with highlighted key data. RP1 only speaks directly to the opposition when instructed. Tracks progress toward the negotiation objective. RP1 emotions and body language must remain neutral and not reveal any insights. Typically, this position is filled by a trusted finance, strategic planning, or analytics person.

Development—Left Position 1 (LP1): LP1 sits immediately to the left of NL in a key *offensive* position. The role is to communicate key observations and suggestions to NL. LP1 notifies the leader when something is leverageable in the discussions. Has preapproval to address the room when reinforcing positive ideas with support points. Can extend other side's ideas when it supports own initiatives. Replies with thought-provoking business-building ideas, "Yes, and we can also...." Exhibits nonverbal positive reactions when momentum is building. Tracks progress to the negotiation overall goal. This person usually has a background in marketing or business development.

Notetaker—Right Position 2 (RP2): RP2 sits immediately to the right of PR1 in a *secondary defensive* position. The role is to take notes and access extensive data such as sales, costs, industry data, and projections. This person sits out of the line of sight and contributes supporting data or performs ad-hoc analysis. They have immediate access to the current proposal, previous contracts, and key details. They are the keeper of *one version of the truth*. Their backgrounds are usually financial accounting, category management, or customer support.

Liaison—Left Position 2 (LP2): LP2 sits immediately to the left of LP1 in a *secondary offensive* position. The role is a qualitative observer on what is and is not working. This person reads the tone and nonverbal cues of the other side. Will be called on to minimize difficulties of any execution obstacles. Even the most absurd idea will be received with a positive response such as "There may be a way to do it." The other side appreciates this person as they demonstrate confidence the agreement will generate positive results. This person knows the other side's organization from top to bottom and has good relationships throughout. If the deal falls apart and feelings are hurt, they will not suffer collateral damage. This person is usually the sales account manager, operations, or customer relations representative.

Freelance Position 3 (FP3): This is a consultant or advisor and sometimes called the *sniper* or *joker*. FP3 sits perpendicular to both NLs. They have a solid industry reputation and have earned the respect of the room. Although not in the line of sight of the leaders, this person may cause distractions throughout the process. Their role is to keep the other side off balance to prevent them from dominating any key issue or gaining a negotiation edge. When their side is losing momentum or the discussion has become unproductive, they will take a piece of information out of context and change the position on the issue. Acknowledge that you have heard their point, but do not validate it or let them add to it. Let the comment lay there for a moment and move to a different topic.

If the meeting is contentious, having this *tough guy* on your side will give you an edge. They know the market and previous deal points better than anyone. Snipers are most effective late in the process when you are losing a zero-sum negotiation. They are highly competent, precise, efficient, and systematic with escalating different points of view into conflicts. Snipers have superior knowledge of industrywide tangential topics such as legal, investor relations, industry relationships, public relations, or human resources. They are usually a semiretired veteran salesperson, ex-CFO, or consultant.

Deal Approver Attendance

If a contentious competitive negotiation is expected, an edge is created by not having the final authority/decision maker in the meetings or available to the other party. Similar to a chess match, don't expose the king or queen too early. Dominating C-suite executives, with their large egos, can get caught-up in the emotion. Decision makers like to control the discussion, which can force an agreement too quickly. Their superior position pressures the other side to see it their way, creating an immovable position or an overly aggressive counter proposal. Decision makers tend to reveal what is really important too early in the process. Also, their presence undermines the negotiating leader's ability to manage the negotiation narrative. It's best to have the final authority join the negotiation *at the end of the process* when quick decisions and compromises are needed to close the deal.

Attorney Attendance

The one attendee who is essential to the negotiation but may need to be excluded from the initial meeting is your attorney. Having your attorney attend the first meeting tends to put the other side on the defensive, which inhibits a free flow of ideas. This forces a competitive negotiation while minimizing collaboration and compromises. If your attorney insists on attending, guide them to say as little as possible, perhaps only responding to legal issues.

Expect your attorney to resist any restrictions on attending or meeting room behavior. Not including your attorney may be perceived as being disrespectful and positions them as second tier or nonessential to the negotiation. Attorneys have the capability to derail a negotiation more than anyone on your team. Be very careful weighing the pros and cons when making the decision on their attendance.

You have no choice but to have your attorney attend if the other side's attorney will be attending. With both attorneys present, be aware all the discussions will be documented and may be used against you later. Attorneys are competitive and inclined to prove they are the superior legal person in the room. That situation is called *out-lawyering* the other side. Managing your attorney during a negotiation is a sensitive and delicate process.

Overcrowded Negotiation Room

If your side of the negotiation table is overcrowded, create an edge by instructing everyone to have an extremely positive attitude. A room filled with positive reinforcement creates momentum and can sway the other side to your favor. However, if the other side significantly outnumbers your side, gain the edge by keeping your team small with only the top guardians of the business attending. With greater numbers, the other side will feel the need to lead the discussion. You can be selective in your reactions. With fewer people present, it is acceptable behavior to ask for more time to respond to the commentary. Guardians tend to be the NL and one support person such as a general manager, general counsel, or a finance executive to deflect attack points.

CHAPTER 4

Negotiating Room Behavior

Know the Expectations and Learn the Etiquette

Negotiation meetings are a forum for an exchange of ideas. Your behavior provokes a response, which creates a reaction, and the process continues until one side signals an end to the discussion. Like any formal business or social gathering, there are expected behaviors and etiquette guidelines that establish a productive environment, leading to a satisfactory result. Poor behavior disrupts the process and can lead to impasses. This can cause a shift from a mutually beneficial outcome to winning short-term results.

Good leaders focus on the negotiation process as much as the outcome. Productive behavior is established by exhibiting *trust, integrity,* and *commitment.* This is accomplished by showing *respect, sincerity,* and *reliability.* The side with the best behavior discipline will gain the edge.

The expectations and etiquette in this section can be applied to internal meetings of your ongoing business interactions. Good behavior is an overlooked and underemphasized skill in business management. Technology has made business communication extremely efficient, but it can lead to misunderstandings and unproductive behavior. Knowing the expectations and following the etiquette will advance your career.

Productive Behavior

The tone of the meeting should be calm and respectful to create a comfortable environment. A temperate voice with a deliberate cadence communicates competence and confidence. It is optimal for both sides to have with the same level of confidence at the beginning of the negotiation.

The leader should discuss the expected behavior with the negotiation team before each meeting. Productive meetings start with a mutually approved agenda with a list of attendees with no surprise appearances. The leader's responsibility is to stay on the agenda and avoid nonessential topics. Arriving late, taking outside calls, or leaving early is bad negotiating room behavior. Arriving on time and staying until the meeting mutually ends shows respect. Consistent good behavior shows a commitment to getting the deal done.

One of the more challenging behaviors is being receptive to an unfavorable term or contrary point. Demonstrating a *willingness to listen to alternatives* and *being flexible* will keep both parties engaged in the negotiation. The tone of the negotiation will change for the worse when one side irrationally holds onto their original position. A rigid position is subconsciously communicated with defensive body language. Looking away, leaning back in the chair, folded arms, clinched fists, furrowed brow, downturned mouth are off-putting, nonverbal behaviors.

Each side comes to the negotiation with emotional baggage that is best left at the door. The leaders cannot allow their personal feelings or ego to get in the way of making a good deal. Neither side needs to like each other, but they must show mutual respect.

Listening Skills

The side with superior listening skills will gain an edge. Show the other side you care and comprehend what they are saying motivates them to continue to reveal their needs and wants. Maintain nonthreatening eye contact and physically write notes on paper. Briefly nod each time they make a point to show you heard them. Jot down a few words as the other side speaks to show you are paying full attention. Do not take notes on a computer, tablet, or phone as it can be viewed as multitasking and presenting a disinterested posture. Try not to interrupt; however, asking a clarifying question after a point is made can reinforce your interest.

Body Language

Speakers subconsciously interpret your body language. Demonstrate your interest by sitting up straight with a slight forward lean. Having a comfortable posture will communicate openness and a lack of threat to the other side. Your face and hands will reveal how your feel about each point being made by the other side. Have a contented expression with relaxed eyebrows and slight smile. Avoid a *determined expression* of furrowed brow, clenched jaw, and downturned mouth. Keep your hands comfortably flat or open on the table. Don't move them while they are speaking. Do not have folded arms or clenched fists, which communicates tension or a lack of receptiveness.

Mirroring

Mirroring has a positive effect on neural transmitters, which creates a comfortable state of mind for negotiating. Following your opponent's physical mannerisms, verbal pacing and tone can create a positive emotional bond. Restating the other side's key points in a positive manner establishes empathic feelings. A genuine smile will encourage the flow of positive enzymes throughout your and your opponent's body. Avoid the forced, disingenuous smile as it will communicate insincerity and dishonesty.

Hosting the Negotiation Meeting

Being the host requires specific behaviors and proper etiquette. The meeting's start time should make it easy to get to the location. Provide as many amenities as possible, especially aesthetically pleasing setting/views, comfortable seating, latest technology, visual aids, and a wide variety of food and beverages. Remember, your environment reflects your values. The meeting should take the other side's company goals into consideration. If the other side is looking for cost savings, a spartan meeting room may be more appropriate. Consider hosting in a neutral site if *the other* side's values differ widely from yours.

Being a proper host requires you to be respectful of the other party's time. When you arrive is indicative of how much respect you have for the other party and the importance of the negotiation. Arriving late is disrespectful and, at best, a petty annoyance. Amateur hosts try to play power games with who can arrive to the meeting room last. Be professional by starting and ending the meetings on time. Some organizations, especially in entertainment and sports, have the most senior person arrive last and leave first. This is off-putting for a potential partner as it conveys the impression that your time is more valuable than theirs. It could put the other side on the offense as you inconvenienced them or tried to show your superiority in an old school way. A suitable defense against this one-upmanship behavior is to be the first to announce, "I have a hard stop at (time)." You know there is a level playing field when the other side responds they want to stop at that time as well. If you feel the absolute need to test your status or leverage, do it at the beginning to set the tone.

Attire

How you dress creates the first impression in the negotiating room. The type of attire sets the tone for the expected formality of communication and negotiation process. Wearing a suit signifies a serious money situation. Some negotiators purposely underdress to show a resistant, noncommittal attitude. How you dress lets everyone know how you feel about yourself and how you want to be perceived.

There are many traditional styles of clothing to consider for the negotiation. You should select clothing that *respects* the room and fits your personality. Consider how long the negotiation is expected, and plan your wardrobe to be consistent with your comfort zone. Do not let the color of your clothing draw unnecessary attention; however, it is acceptable to have bold, bright color accents such as a tie, scarf, or socks. Dressing one-level above your counterparts communicates success and expectations for a high standard of conduct.

Unproductive Behaviors

An erroneous belief is effective negotiating leaders are tough, fast-talking, aggressive, and unrelenting. You cannot reach an agreement by forcing your will on the other side. The desire to get favorable results quickly forces the other side to stake an early rigid position, which leads to unproductive behavior.

Certain behaviors or responses should be avoided throughout the negotiation. Humor, especially sarcasm, is too risky in a negotiation. It has the potential to set an unproductive tone and may offend someone.

Minimize the use of analogies to explain a complex situation. It is a lazy method to address a problem. Nobody ever solved a problem by using an analogy because the listeners tend to focus on the fit aspect of the analogy and not the actual solution.

Avoid eating while either side is speaking as your habits can be a distraction. If a meal is served during the negotiation, it is best to take a break from the discussion to eat. While eating, have social conversations that avoid politics, religion, and anything about the Kardashians. You should have done your homework on the personal lives of the other side. Their interests should be the topic of conversation while eating.

How to Disagree

If you disagree while a point is being made, it is best to show a neutral facial expression rather than a grimace. A negative shake of the head is one of the worst listening behaviors when the other side is speaking. Write down the point of disagreement and wait until the other side has finished speaking to communicate your opinion. It is more productive to address, in priority order, all your points of disagreement at the end of their monolog versus having multiple interruptions. Repetitively objecting to each of their points pushes them into a defensive stance. At the end, address each point of disagreement in a calm manner and in the form of a passive question seeking clarity such as "Is that the market price?" or "How did you derive the order size being at that level?"

Managing Tension

Skilled negotiators keep the other side comfortable throughout the negotiation. Reducing the other side's anxiety or *threat of losing* will establish a stable foundation for a productive negotiation. Knocking the other side off-balance can be a good tactic if used sparingly. It works best for a one-time only negotiation but will fail as a mid-to-long-term tactic. One-upmanship can escalate into a tit-for-tat game and eventually lead to an impasse. You will notice when you have gone too far when the other side responds with a harder "shove back" to regain equal footing. This competitive action creates rigid responses and reduces trust.

Research suggests humans can only sit for 90 minutes before becoming physically uncomfortable. That is why, most movies and TV programs are less than two hours. Be prepared to take a break when you see these signs of fatigue. Schedule breaks and take them. Don't be the toughest person in the room by having marathon negotiating sessions. You are not gaining an advantage making the other side uncomfortable. Give them a break!

It is easy to spot how the other side becomes stressed and relieves it through their physical rituals. Allow these annoying personal behaviors during the process. Disrupting these rituals will increase their stress and make them less cooperative.

Recognizing Stress-Reducing Behaviors

- Drinking coffee, eating snacks
- Tapping feet, fingers, or pen
- Cracking knuckles, playing with hair, licking/biting lips
- Clenching hands, twitching legs
- Shuffling papers, doodling on a pad
- Mumbling to oneself
- Picking at nails
- Playing with rings, watch, or bracelet

Negotiation Room Behavior Checklist

Behaviors to Avoid

- ❑ Decision maker tardiness or inconsistent attendance
- ❑ Attendance of someone not on the meeting invitation
- ❑ Being overconfident a deal will get done
- ❑ Irrationally holding to the original offer or current situation
- ❑ Allowing personal feelings or ego to get in the way
- ❑ Escalating conflict or bad behavior
- ❑ Defensive body language
- ❑ Having confidentiality leaks
- ❑ Constant interruptions
- ❑ Not staying on the agenda
- ❑ Comments supported with faulty data or bad information
- ❑ Ignoring parts of discussions
- ❑ Trying too hard to win every deal term
- ❑ Using sarcasm or bad humor
- ❑ Using analogies or hypothetical situations
- ❑ Annoying personal habits
- ❑ Surprising the other side with a new term or proposal late in the negotiation

CHAPTER 5

Negotiation Preparation

How to Gain the Early Edge

Great preparation enables you to identify key issues in advance and puts you in a position to outperform the negotiation. Completing the necessary analyses in the preparation phase allows for rational and timely decision making, which mitigates the emotional roller coaster of a negotiation.

The preparation starts with receiving the LOI that includes the pillars of the agreement: product, length of agreement, geography, and cost. The agreement length and the geography tend to be discussed and agreed to prior to the LOI. The *battlefield terms* of most negotiations are the product/service and the cost. How well you prepare these terms gives you the initial opportunity to gain the edge.

Create the Battlefield Map

The first preparation step is building a strategic map identifying the goal and objective, needs and wants, strength and vulnerabilities, and potential alternative actions to the deal. This *battlefield map* estimates and compares the initial positions of the two parties and begins the strategy development.

Comparison of Goals and Objectives

The negotiation goal is the qualitative value of how you want your organization to be viewed internally and externally. A common goal is a description of the desired company image or standing in the industry. An example of goals starts with theses phrases, "To be the best in…," "To be the market leader in…," or "To compete with the best…." In the first section of the map, confirm your goal and assign a qualitative value. The value describes the perceived strength of the goal: strong/neutral/ weak, good/better/best, or low/medium/high.

Then, insert your estimate of the other side's negotiation goal and assign a qualitative value. Compare the values. The difference is a *negotiation gap*. If they are similar or complementary with a small gap, the negotiation can expect to go smoothly. If the negotiation gap is large, the negotiation may be difficult. The gap is an early indication which side has the edge. Now you can begin to prepare which strategy to utilize.

Do the same procedure for the negotiating objectives of the two organizations. This financial metric is sometimes referred to as the *overall value of the deal* or *deal worth*. If the negotiation objective has a fixed value, expect a zero-sum or win–lose distributive negotiation. A *competitive strategy* is best suited for negotiations with a fixed value objective. If there is the potential for fluctuation in the values, expect a mutually beneficial, *grow the pie* integrative negotiation. A *collaborative strategy* is best used in this situation. If one side's negotiation objective value is significantly greater, then a *compromise strategy* is best utilized.

Negotiation Battlefield Map Goals and Objectives				
Your Key Terms	**Your Estimate**	**Negotiation Gap**	**Their Estimate**	**Their Key Terms**
Negotiation Goal				Negotiation Goal
Negotiation Objective	$	$	$	Negotiation Objective

Figure 5.1 Negotiation battlefield map goals and objectives chart

Key Term Priorities and Values

The next step is to identify the key terms and set a financial value as either a revenue generator or a cost reduction. Do not include any term that cannot assign a quantitative value such as company image.

Determine the importance to the organization by categorizing the terms as either your top (*needs*) or lower (*wants*) priorities. Then, rank the order from most important to least important. Do the same for the other side's terms. You can get an indication of their values and priorities from their opening offer, industry reporting, or consultants. Identify the areas that are aligned. These are the agreement's *common terms*.

Compare each sides values to determine the *key terms negotiation gap*. If the priorities match, you can expect a straightforward, methodical negotiation. If the priorities are different, the negotiation will have opportunities for trade-offs and may take longer than expected. The gap will determine which side has the edge for each term. Now you can select *the best strategy for each term*.

The total of the term values measures how close you are to getting an agreement. The number can also be used to answer the management question, "How is the negotiation going?" or "How close is the deal?"

Negotiation Battlefield Map Key Term Priorities and Values				
Your Key Terms	**Your Estimate**	**Negotiation Gap**	**Their Estimate**	**Their Key Terms**
Needs: Top Priority Terms				Needs: Top Priority Terms
#1	$	$	$	#1
#2	$	$	$	#2
#3	$	$	$	#3
Subtotal	$	$	$	Subtotal
Wants: Lower Priority Terms				Wants: Lower Priority Terms
#1	$	$	$	#1
#2	$	$	$	#2
#3	$	$	$	#3
Subtotal	$	$	$	Subtotal
TOTAL DEAL VALUE				**TOTAL DEAL VALUE**

Figure 5.2 Negotiation battlefield map key terms and priorities values chart

Selecting the Optimal Strategy: Compete | Collaborate | Compromise

The mapped battlefield enables you to set your strategy. All three strategies can be used on different deal points as the negotiation evolves. One strategy will eventually dominate. Choosing the best one at the optimal time will get you a negotiation edge.

If the negotiation gap gives you an edge, you have the competitive advantage. Treat the term as a win/lose proposition using the *competitive strategy*. Hold your position as the other side will attempt to collaborate to soften your position. Show some interest in collaborating to get the other side to give you key information or trade-off opportunities. When you have a decisive edge, make the other side compromise and move on.

If the negotiation gap gives the other side the edge, they have the competitive advantage. Try to use a *collaborative strategy* to get them to trade-off other terms in the deal or share information that may benefit you later in the negotiation. Do not go to a *compromise strategy* unless it will close the deal. You will lose value compromising too early in the negotiation.

If there is only a small negotiation gap, a *collaborative strategy* may work best. A collaborative strategy shares information, data, and ideas to create the best deal possible for all parties. Let the other side know you want to work together to make the key terms even better. Starting with similarly valued terms will create momentum early in the negotiation.

Mapping Deal Terms (Example)				
Terms	Our Value	Edge	Their Value	Strategy
Term #1	$100	$30	$70	Compete—High Priority
Term #2	$90	$10	$80	Collaborate—Moderate Priority
Term #3	$80	($5)	$85	Compromise—Low Priority
Total Terms	$270	$35	$235	Higher total value for the deal

Figure 5.3 Mapping deal terms example

Expect to continually update both side's values after every negotiation meeting. The strategies may change due to a counter proposal or market condition volatility in each side's term values. Providing written updates along the way establishes a record of changes, which will minimize confusion, frustration, and irrational responses.

Comparison of Strength and Vulnerabilities

Continue developing the battlefield map by identifying the strengths and vulnerabilities for both sides. The source can come from your strategic planning department, performance reviews, or external industry sources in these categories:

- Personnel
- Marketing
- Sales
- Operations
- Financial strength/access to capital
- Business size/market position
- Public perception/brand image
- Industry knowledge
- Flexibility/speed to market/adaptability

Once you have your list, decide how to measure these aspects of your business. Assign either a quantitative or qualitative factor for each side. This can be a descriptive comparison such as *advantage/disadvantage*, low/medium/high, good/better/best, or a quantifiable comparison such as a five-point scale (1–5, low to high). The gap between the two side's values will show which side has the negotiation edge. From there, determine which strategy fits best with the strength and vulnerability. A competitive strategy tends to work best with strengths and collaborative strategy works best with vulnerabilities. Save the compromise strategy toward the end of the negotiation.

The final factor is whether either side has an alternative to completing a deal. Does one side have a stronger benefit if the deal is not completed? One of the best negotiating edges is to have an alternative plan to the potential agreement to achieve your goal and objective.

Negotiation Battlefield Map Strengths and Vulnerabilities				
Your Key Terms	Your Estimate	Negotiation Gap	Their Estimate	Their Key Terms
Strengths				Strengths
#1				#1
#2				#2
#3				#3
Vulnerabilities				Vulnerabilities
#1				#1
#2				#2
#3				#3
Viable Alternative Actions				Viable Alternative Actions

Figure 5.4 Negotiation battlefield map strengths and vulnerabilities chart

Develop the Engagement Plan

The leader will develop a negotiation timetable to ensure there is adequate time and resources to complete the negotiation process and achieve a satisfactory outcome. The development of the engagement plan begins with estimating how many internal meetings will be needed before, during, and after the negotiation. A difficult negotiation will be time consuming and require more meetings. There are three groups that need their own meeting schedule: negotiating team, stakeholders, and the other side.

Negotiating Team Meetings

Negotiation rehearsals, like athletic practices, are to ensure everyone on the negotiation team understands and performs their roles. Every important negotiation meeting needs a rehearsal. Every participant must know what is to be accomplished for the meeting and stay within their area of expertise. How ineffective would a team be if the tight end wanted to play quarterback for a few plays? In the same sense, you do not want your financial analyst debating legal terms with the other side.

Those who tend to veer off strategy with their comments should be told firmly upfront there is zero tolerance for that behavior. Visible conflict between the leader and a team member can give the other side an edge. It is better to identify and remove the uncooperative staff member before the negotiation. Removing them during the process will create an opportunity for the removed person to undermine the negotiations internally and externally.

Stakeholder Meetings

The number of stakeholders and the complexity of deal terms will determine how many internal meetings are required. A complex agreement will need more meetings to analyze the terms throughout the negotiation. A large number of internal stakeholders will require more meetings to inform, influence, and gain support. Stakeholders need constant reinforcement that their needs are being prioritized. It is critical to get their feedback before the negotiation starts. Individual meetings allow you to get their prospective and create the impression that their needs are a top priority. This can be time-consuming for the leader, who may want to delegate some of the lesser stakeholder meetings.

Avoid the strategic error of trying to save time by having all the stakeholders meet at one time. The negotiation leader is vulnerable in a multiple stakeholder meeting, especially when there are unsatisfied stakeholders voicing their displeasure. Avoid disgruntled stakeholders forming a coalition to force their special interests into the negotiation. Don't create an occasion where they can band together and bully you into a bad position because once they do, it is difficult to overcome.

Meetings With the Other Side

Once the internal staff and stakeholder meeting schedules are set, determine the required number of meetings with the other side. Setting meeting dates all the way up to the deadline will ensure there is no break in the process. Never break an appointment regardless of how the discussions are going. Negotiators need to keep talking despite seemingly insurmountable differences. Keeping the dialog going is like a patient on life support. If you stop meeting, the negotiation will die.

The leader's mantra is *keep communicating*—no shutdowns. Express meaningful assurances you will deliver superior product or service in all aspects of the agreement. It's important to maintain productive relationships among all parties during negotiation. Reinforce this will be a productive long-lasting relationship. Here are two examples of how to communicate your intent to perform at the highest levels:

- Wal-Mart buying team philosophy, "Let us know when we are not being good partners."
- Warner Bros. ex-CEO Kevin Tsujihara philosophy, "The deal terms don't matter if we don't enjoy working together."

If the process starts to break down, then meet with a smaller group. If the situation deteriorates further, then have only the leaders meet. A useful method to resolve an impasse is to have only the leaders meet outside of the scheduled negotiation meetings. There is a hierarchy of eating occasions for impasse resolution: breakfast when discussions are becoming unproductive, lunch when the meetings are going very poorly, and dinner when the situation has reached an impasse.

When setting up the social meeting, pick up the expenses to show you are a good host. The relative cost of establishing a relationship is worth the investment. Strive to subtly control the discussion by preparing a script of questions and solutions. Collaborative and compromise strategies are needed at this time. Your goal is to leave with a solution to the impasse. The place should be in a pleasant environment so that the other party will feel relaxed. Most hard-working executives appreciate the break from their office and look forward to being in a nice setting. It is hard to be upset or tense surrounded by palm trees, views of water or rolling hills while eating a high-quality meal. This will also mitigate any desire to leave if the discussions don't progress smoothly. The time and location of the meeting should be highly confidential. The optics of excessive spending should be avoided, especially if the new deal will have significant cost savings, including employee layoffs.

Confidentiality Guidelines

Flat organizations have created a premium on establishing and maintaining productive long-term relationships. However, this structure increases the risk for information leaks. Confidentiality is very important to the communication plan in a negotiation. The leader must educate the team early in the process on the importance of confidentiality. Parsing out information and updates should be on a *need-to-know* basis. When colleagues ask a negotiation team member how a negotiation is going, the appropriate response is "What is your need to know: social or business?" If it is business status, the leader is the only person permitted to disseminate information. If it is a social question, then the answer should only be a brief optimistic assessment of the negotiation's status.

Set Contractual Protections

Contractual protections not only secure your fair participation in any upside, but more importantly, protect your downside in any possible scenario. Don't be overwhelmed by all the scenarios of what could possibly go wrong. The legal language should provide some wiggle room to renegotiate a worst-case scenario. This step requires an attorney who knows your industry well enough to identify and protect against all the potential adverse situations. Consider outsourcing this part of the negotiation's paperwork to a contract expert to draft the final agreement. The protection clauses should cover the following:

- Representations: Assertions made at the time of the signed agreement
- Covenants: Basic promises or expected conduct in the normal course of business
- Conditions: Outside factors impacting the agreement
- Indemnities: Circumstances for which an injured party may be reimbursed

Negotiation Preparation Checklist

- ❑ Are you personally committed to establishing and keeping the relationship?
- ❑ Do you respect the company and the people on the other side?
- ❑ Can I work with the other side?
- ❑ Have you gathered and analyzed all the terms of the deal?
- ❑ Are your projections as accurate as can be?
- ❑ What market conditions will change your projections?
- ❑ Have you identified all the obstacles?
- ❑ Do you have the necessary resources to complete and execute the agreement?
- ❑ Do you have the support of your organization's management?
- ❑ Have you identified all the stakeholders, and how they will benefit/lose?
- ❑ What extra work will the stakeholders need to perform if an agreement is signed?
- ❑ What is the probability on reaching a favorable or mutually beneficial agreement?

Preparation Work Sheet

Negotiation Battlefield Map				
Your Key Terms	**Your Estimate**	**Negotiation Gap**	**Their Estimate**	**Their Key Terms**
Negotiation Goal				Negotiation Goal
Negotiation Objective	$	$	$	Negotiation Objective
Needs: Top Priority Terms				Needs: Top Priority Terms
#1	$	$	$	#1
#2	$	$	$	#2
#3	$	$	$	#3
Subtotal	$	$	$	Subtotal
Wants: Lower Priority Terms				Wants: Lower Priority Terms
#1	$	$	$	#1
#2	$	$	$	#2
#3	$	$	$	#3
Subtotal	$	$	$	Subtotal
Strengths				Strengths
#1				#1
#2				#2
#3				#3
Vulnerabilities				Vulnerabilities
#1				#1
#2				#2
#3				#3
Viable Alternative Actions				Viable Alternative Actions

Figure 5.5 Negotiation battlefield map

CHAPTER 6

Negotiation Psychology

How to Read and React to Gain the Edge

Motivations and Decision-Making

The ability to understand the other side's motivations and decision-making process is an essential skill in a negotiation. Understanding *what* the other side is communicating can be confusing, especially when emotions and deadlines are involved. Many studies have quantified the process of communication being 70 percent nonverbal, 20 percent tone, and only 10 percent content. The ability to comprehend another person's actions, tone, and words must overcome stress, physical distractions, poor word choice, and irrational responses. To be a successful negotiator, one must decipher the other's side position and provide an optimal response.

This tactic can be applied to other areas of your career. Doing a *deep-dive* on people you are meeting or have an impact on your profession will enable you to understand their motivations and decision making, which will improve your relationships. There is a saying in the legal profession: know the judge as well as the law—the same applies with negotiations. Know their leader as well as the deal terms.

Profile the Other Side's Leader

Your negotiation strategy will be influenced by the other side's leadership style. Understanding the other side's leader creates a negotiation edge. Recognizing the type of person negotiating across the table enables you to adapt your communication and engage successfully.

Begin the process by learning as much as possible about the other side's leader. Develop a complete profile by researching their personal life, education, job performance, hobbies, and colleagues. Successful executives tend to rely on skills developed early in their careers. They will repeat the behavior of their successes and avoid those of their failures. Although it is sometimes better to outsource, the process of profiling has been enhanced by technology. How does the other side's leader communicate and make decisions? How does it compare to your leader's skill and style? Similar styles increase the probability of a successful negotiation.

There are numerous methods to profile negotiators. Most profiling techniques have a four-quadrant process identifying four key behaviors. The primary quadrant indicates how the leader will perform in most situations. The secondary or subquadrant identifies how the leader will perform under stress such as when the negotiation reaches an impasse. The third factor is the *variability spectrum* or *chameleon* factor, which indicates the flexibility of the leader's style and the ability to change in different situations. The following provides a method to evaluate negotiation leadership styles. Leadership attributes ranked on a scale of 1 (low) to 5 (high).

Leadership Style Comparison

Leadership Traits (1–5)	Your Leader	Their Leader	Difference
1. Decides by Intuition			
2. Decides by Data			
3. Competitive			
4. Collaborative			
5. Proactive			
6. Reactive			
7. Social Skills			
8. Straight Shooter			
9. Evasive			
10. Trustworthy			
11. Optimistic			
12. Talkative			
13. Secretive			
14. Energy Level			

15. Organization Standing
16. Industry Network

Determine how the two leaders compare. Knowing how both leaders behave will enable you to understand how they make decisions. Adjust your style to fit the other side's leader. Don't expect the other side's leader to adjust to your behavior. This preparation will mitigate a major source of frustration when the other side does not behave as expected.

The other side's negotiation team can be expected to follow their leader's behavior. It can be revealing when someone on the other side does not follow the leader's example. Determine the specific conflict between the leader and the team member. Finding the weak link in the negotiation team can be exploited to create an edge.

Negotiation Leader Types

Organizational behavior specialists have developed numerous methods to profile executive psychological profiles. I have developed six negotiation leader profiles based on how they prefer to receive information, make decisions, and communicate.

The Hammer

Their deals get done, but on their terms. Hammers don't waste time. They favor a competitive strategy but will tolerate a shift to a collaborative strategy in nonessential areas. They come with predetermined positions and are resistant to compromise. Hammers expect their previous successes will translate to this situation. They take a superior posture and may even try to mentor you during the negotiation. Resist being offended by their condescending attitude. Hammer's favorite expressions are, "If I were you...," "What you need to understand is...," and "This is what you need to do...."

Hammers are not concerned about your position and will appear uncooperative early in the negotiation. You can stroke their egos by telling them how right they are on select topics. Expect awkward humor. Their attempt for empathy will come from feint self-deprecating commentary. It is best not to engage or acknowledge it.

There is a positive side of dealing with a Hammer. They have the authority to make the deal and don't waste time. Compromises come begrudgingly at the end to close the deal. Negotiating with a Hammer is like a boxing match. You need to avoid getting hit early and often. Your best defense is patience and a firm resolve.

A Hammer's traits are a large ego, confidence, impatience, aggression, opinionated, determined, risk-taker, and fast-paced decision making. Their backgrounds are commonly senior executive/CEO with an advanced degree or a proud self-made founder/owner. Expect both to have the complete support of their organizations and board of directors. Hammers are best at negotiating short-term or one-time agreements.

The Party Host

They want everyone to feel good about the negotiation process as well as the outcome as it enhances their stature. They like to present the *big picture* and be the first to take the high ground by announcing their positions are for the greater good. Their preferred negotiation strategy is collaborative and will offer compromises early in the process. They tend to reveal their needs early. Their staff will try to save their leader from a bad deal. Party Hosts will solicit input from all stakeholders before and during the negotiation to be able to read the room effectively.

Party Hosts make decisions based on intuition and rely on feelings over facts. The negotiation focus will be on sharing, harmony, and creating solutions. Their high social IQ may lead you to underestimate their intelligence or strategic thinking. They are excellent manipulators who know how to frame the issues and motivate others to perform. They are often perceived as strategic, big picture, visionary, flexible, cooperative, warm, friendly, sensitive, benevolent, empathetic, and risk avoidance. Negotiations led by a Party Host tend to go well but can take longer than expected to get a final agreement.

Their weaknesses are lack of preparation and attention to detail. They tend to disregard data when responding to a competitive strategy. Complex issues will not be fully discussed to your satisfaction because the Party Host wants to move away from the details. An abundance of data and methodical linear pace will frustrate them. They will suggest putting these issues to the side for later. This avoidance behavior causes problems as it creates too many loose ends. Stay disciplined and committed to resolving each issue before moving to the next topic.

Party Hosts tend to avoid direct conflict when the negotiation falters. This is where you must protect yourself. When at an impasse, the Party Host will denigrate your position from their perceived higher ground. They are very adept at *kicking dirt on your shoes*. You don't see it, but others will. When not in negotiating meetings, they are defending their position with others and subtly turning others against you. Stakeholders and the industry players will believe you're the problem as the Party Host is such a nice, reasonable person.

The biggest downside to a Party Host is they tend not to have the authority to approve the deal. They often report to either an analytical supervisor or a diverse group such as a board of directors. The deal-approving entity gets to observe the battle from afar and call the shots. They appreciate the Party Host's ability to bring people together and gain consensus. Party Hosts are best for negotiating ongoing relationships and contract extensions in stable markets.

The Brainiac

This is the smartest person in the room but lacks interpersonal skills. They keep the negotiation moving but tend to struggle getting to a conclusion. They need others to work the room to progress toward an agreement with data and rational thought. Their methodical decision-making process is pragmatic, detail-oriented, fact-based, and multidirectional. They use a competitive strategy that is entirely based on their data. Brainiacs believe there is no need to compromise or collaborate as the numbers will lead to an optimal conclusion. They tend to wait for all the data to become available and take the time to *think through* the issue before moving onto the next topic. They are comfortable with conflict perceiving it as only a difference in the interpretation of the data. Brainiacs enjoy using their superior intellect and deductive reasoning to resolve different POVs. They value competency, productivity, accuracy, efficiency, and do not like to go back to previous decisions unless new data are presented.

They are perceived as functional, process-oriented, competent, productive, efficient, autonomous, calm, uncaring, deliberate, strong-willed, and comfortable with measured risk. The facts of the situation will drive the negotiation, but the need for data will make progress time-consuming. Do not expect them to readily share information. You have to ask directly for it. Their vulnerabilities are new processes, emerging markets, effecting change, resolving subjective issues, indirect confrontation, and social skills. Their backgrounds tend to be CFO, attorney, or engineer with advance degrees in finance, accounting, law, or engineering.

The Carnival Barker

They enjoy leading the negotiation from the center of the action and being perceived as a well-connected mover and shaker. They will use a collaborative strategy with a willingness to compromise to make progress and conclude the negotiation. They will verbally challenge you to compromise on key issues. Expect them to comment on every aspect of the discussions, often repeating their viewpoints. Barkers believe their ability to make a quick decision is a sign of high intelligence. They are always selling their ideas and thrive in a changing environment. They utilize emotion and intuition to make decisions. They tend not to gather their own data and need information from external channels.

Barkers have a big impact early in the negotiations but tend to fade as the discussions continue. When losing a discussion point, they will grasp a small truth and expand on it. Barkers tend to communicate hyperbole as fact. They are vulnerable to misstatements or incorrect information. If this happens, do not let it pass because it will become a fact. Press the Barker for specific information and facts to support their claims. Don't let them take your statements to the extreme to discredit your premise. Address the exaggeration immediately with your data and defend your point to resolution.

Barkers tend to get impatient with established processes and like to make change for change's sake. They will stray off topic in longer meetings. It can be hard to pin them down on specific actions or agreements. Gain the edge from controlling the information by documenting the discussions and distributing the meeting's follow-up notes. Barkers can be described as adaptable, daring, high social IQ, friendly, expressive, overbearing, fearless, high energy, and well-connected. Their common backgrounds are revenue generation, sales, or business development.

The Unrelenting Grinder

The Unrelenting Grinder Horror! (UGH!), the most difficult and challenging of all negotiation styles. You need to be in a good mental state to negotiate with an Unrelenting Grinder. They will test all aspects of leadership. Ensure you have complete support from your supervisor before you engage a negotiation with a Grinder.

Grinders utilize a competitive strategy, rarely compromising or collaborating. They are most effective at negotiating one time, distributive zero sum, short-term agreements. They will try to win every topic, issue, or term. Every discussion point is debated and challenged from all sides. If you give on one point, do not expect to get the next one. If you win a point, they will go back to a previous point to renegotiate it.

Their incredible negotiation stamina can wear you down and push you into a compromise. Their negotiations progress slowly and painfully. It will challenge your motivation to complete the agreement. Keep your negotiation goals and objective in mind to avoid frustration and the desire to walk away.

The most successful Grinders hide their style. They start by being pleasant and overly optimistic about getting to a deal. They will be agreeable to the negotiation setups such as dates, times, and locations. They want you to be relaxed and comfortable so that you will let your guard down. Nothing seems to be an issue for them until you get in the negotiation room. This is where they turn into negotiation beasts.

Your best strategy against a Grinder is to prepare and win the data battle on every issue. Showing you have superior data early in the negotiation will change the tone and pacing. Anticipate the size and quality of their data and make sure you have more and better information. They will try to invalidate your data, so they need to be current and accurate. Do not engage them until your information is superior.

Another good defensive tactic is to keep a running record of progress by documenting discussions, key issues, and approvals. Seeing progress will keep your emotions in check when the going gets toughest. The negotiating team will need to be on their best behavior as they will be tested. The team needs to stay in their roles of providing information and data at key points while resisting the urge to jump into the fray. Grinders are great at twisting information to their advantage when your junior team member speaks out of turn. It is safest to have the smallest negotiating team in the room with a Grinder.

Starting the negotiation with a firm deadline is a necessity with Grinders. Without one, the negotiation would continue until you are beaten down into submission. You can expect to see a change in the Grinder's behavior when a deadline approaches. They will reprioritize the terms and attack the most important ones first, creating an opportunity to trade for the less important terms. Be prepared to make quick decisions as there is a lot of activity right before the deadline.

Do not let the other side's behavior sway your decision making. Always know the current quantitative value of the negotiation compared to your negotiation objective. This will keep your focus on how close the projected outcome of the agreement is to your objective and prevent you from walking away too early in the process. Ask yourself if there is a path to an agreement. If not, when is the optimal time to leave the fight? Grinders will not read your feelings or show empathy. Indicating you are unhappy with the lack of progress will have no impact on them. Fight the urge to communicate you may walk away from the negotiation to get them to change their behavior. It will not work. The walk-away tactic is only effective with Grinders at the very end of the negotiation.

Even if the deadline passes, you can expect the Grinder to re-engage to win the deal. Do not allow them to reopen a negotiation unless they give you everything you need. If you reopen and fail to get an agreement, your reputation will take a hit as they will position you as irrational and being difficult.

The positive aspect of negotiating with a Grinder is a great sense of accomplishment completing an agreement. Grinders will bring out the best of your negotiation skills. The deal itself will have a high probability of success as all the terms have been examined and re-examined by both sides over a long period of time. You and your team can be proud of your achievement. Make sure you celebrate the result and take some time off. It will take weeks to decompress after an UGH! of a negotiation.

The Sage

The Sage is a senior executive who holds an esteemed position in the organization or the industry. They have a lot of experience to lead the current negotiation but rarely have the authority to approve the deal. Know the backstory and motivation of the Sage as some are unhappy not having authority and being in a *nonoperational* position. The Sage's ego will let you know where they disagree with their organization about the negotiation.

The Sage will offer oversimplified and pragmatic views of the situation. They are motivated to maintain the status quo as any changes will threaten their standing in the organization or industry. The Sage always comes prepared and feels most comfortable with their proven process. They use familiar methodologies to solve impasses and bring people together. Although their tone can be condescending at times, always show your respect. Their weakness is not being able to deviate from the current process, so new situations and terms tend to be avoided. Your best offense is to have an abundance of current data to counter the Sage's past experiences. Utilize a "That was then, this is now" strategy when engaging a Sage. Traditions and business etiquette are important to them. When the need to confront them arises, show respect and softly contradict their points.

Versatility Factor: The V-factor is the ability of a negotiation leader to change their communication style or decision-making process over the course of the negotiation. Good leaders have a high V-factor, allowing them to adapt to the situation. Reaching an impasse or an approaching deadline may require one of the leaders to change behavior. Observe if the other side's leader has high/medium/low versatility to adapt to the situation. If not, then you will have to be the one who adapts to their behavior. A common cause of reaching a negotiation impasse is when both leaders are unwilling or incapable of changing their negotiation style. The most common solutions after long impasse are to walk away from the deal or change one of the leaders.

Reading and Reacting to Verbal Cues

Successful negotiations have uninterrupted productive discussions. This is achieved when both sides engage in a calm and rational manner. Mirroring good behavior creates a bond that diffuses tension over the course of a negotiation. Expect the discussions to become more difficult as the deadline approaches. The stress of an advancing deadline may cause irrational behavior such as raised voices, abrupt interruptions, sarcastic comments, stubbornly holding one's position, or being unresponsive.

You have reached an impasse when the other side repeats their position using the same words, but with an escalation in volume. Speaking with a louder voice does not make anyone understand better or change their POV. It's the fear of the not getting a critical need. A louder tone reveals a vulnerability, which gives you an edge.

The key to getting through a difficult negotiation phase is not letting their bad behavior impact your emotions. Bad behavior in negotiations comes from uncontrolled stress and anxiety. Listen carefully, although it can be difficult. Determine the true meaning of what is being said. Being a good listener during a stressful time is hard to do. The first inclination is to quickly strike back with equal or more force. Be observant, patient, and let the other side vent. At the right time, respond to them in a non-threatening manner with your understanding of the issue and ask them to acknowledge or confirm it. Try not to escalate their emotions. Continue to reinforce you want a deal by the deadline.

Reading and Reacting to Nonverbal Cues

Reading nonverbal cues starts with your opponent's physical behavior in the initial meetings. Ordinary, repeated actions establish their baseline behavior. When stress is introduced into the meeting, they will exhibit extraordinary behavior such as shifting their sitting posture, accentuating hand gestures, or facial expressions. These actions indicate a high-value topic for them. Once you know their priorities, leverage them and pick the best time to counter-offer this term.

The face is the main communication device for nonverbal cues. It is the only part of the body where muscle is attached to skin and not bone. Facial muscles can react involuntarily to visual stimuli before one has time to think about a reaction. Extreme reactions are readable after a baseline is established. Look for a flash of movement in the eyebrows or mouth areas. It will indicate if they are going to compete, collaborate, or compromise.

Psychologists have categorized human behavior in various situations. By labeling these human behaviors, one can recognize the reaction, understand the basic feeling, and respond accordingly. Following is a list of common negotiation emotional and tactical reactions to understand and utilize.

Negotiation Cues Checklist

❑ Batoning: Making a point.

❑ Steepling: Feeling superior.

❑ Hand to chin: Judging you and the issue.

❑ The Flinch—extreme negative reaction.

❑ The Emotional Barrage: Over-the-top reaction. "You always/ never…"

❑ The Sob Story or Victim Card: "I am so beaten down. I doubt I can proceed."

❑ The Squeeze: Threat of a better deal elsewhere.

❑ The Nibble: Asking for a little extra usually right before the signing of a deal.

❑ The Escalation: Asking for more each time a term is discussed.

❑ The Ultimatum: Take it or leave it.

❑ The Delay: Resetting the deadline due to unforeseen circumstances.

❑ The Assumptive Close: Prematurely assumes the deal is done.

❑ The Lowball: Rationalizes a very low offer.

❑ The Negotiator Change: New person takes over responsibility for the deal.

❑ The Straw Demand: Asking for something new or different but of little true value. Usually introduced at an impasse or the very end of a negotiation.

(Source: Ed Brodow)

CHAPTER 7

Negotiation Strategy

How to Compete, Collaborate, and Compromise

Negotiation Types

There are two negotiation types, with each having different processes and strategies. One negotiation type, *distributive* is a highly competitive lose–win, zero-sum situation with confidential discussions involving a small group of people. The other type, *integrative* is collaborative with shared information making a mutually beneficial agreement for large groups.

Sometimes, a negotiation can evolve into a hybrid of distributive and integrative types. One side can change their strategy during the process because of a new term, new leader, or market condition volatility. There can also be compromises in both negotiation types in order to trade off terms.

To have a successful negotiation, you need to identify which type of negotiation you are entering and adapt your corresponding strategies: compete, collaborate, or compromise.

Two-Party Distributive Negotiation

Distributive negotiations are sometimes called *zero sum, fixed value,* or *win/lose* because one side will gain more value than the other side. The total value of the transaction is fixed, and each side sets their own fixed value for the agreement. A distributive negotiation is *position oriented* and tends to utilize a *competitive strategy*. Typically, there is a trade-off for control or ownership of assets or services in exchange for a monetary value. Price tends to be the focus. The side with control of the asset or service tends to have the negotiation edge unless it is a commodity. A two-party distributive negotiation typically starts with one side taking a position and presenting their rationale with support data. The discussion will highlight the benefits to the other side for moving closer to this position. There is minimal collaboration or sharing of private data. It is critical during this time to read the other side's verbal and nonverbal cues to determine leverage points. Each of the following factors can be used to gain the edge on the deal. Which side wants:

- More than the other side
- The least amount of risk
- The deadline to happen sooner
- The overall deal to cover a shorter time period

Successful distributive negotiators tend to start with competitive strategies but will utilize compromise strategies near the end to close the deal. Impasses are prevalent when negotiators are unyielding and only focus on defending their position. The less experienced negotiators tend to arrive at a *take it or leave it* position too early in the negotiation. The better distributive negotiators see the deal from the other side's position and try to satisfy their *needs* and *wants* in a priority order.

The first offer and counteroffer are critical as they reveal initial positions and frame the negotiation. One side may rush to frame the negotiation when the marketplace is relatively new or highly volatile. Each side keeps their interests confidential, except when creating leverage by overtly or subtly revealing potential alternative buyers/sellers. Walking away or pursuing other bidders is called the *best alternative to a negotiated agreement* (BATNA) and was made popular by Harvard professor Max Baverman.

Multiparty Distributive Negotiation

Auctions are most effective for multiparty, time-sensitive distributive negotiations. Technology has made auctions the most common form of distributive negotiation. Understanding the various types of auctions and their distinct processes will provide your best outcome. The periphery of the auction is where the auction is won. The key to success is to prepare better than the competition. Often times, the information that is supposed to be confidential leaks to the well-informed parties. Following are the most popular auction types:

English Auction (aka Ascending Bid or Open Outcry)

Bidders sequentially declare a commitment to a higher price, and the bidding stops when no other entity increases from the previous bid. It is the most common type because the transparent price and bid competition usually generates the most revenue for an asset. The auctioneer can influence the outcome by reading the room and playing to the competitor's emotions. The key component of a winning bidding strategy is making the competition know you are highly motivated to win the asset. Sit where you will be noticed and top the previous bid with quick verbal conviction. Display confidence and an enjoyment of the bidding competition. Do your preparation early as possible on the value of the asset, payment terms, and other costs associated with the winning bid such as storage, shipping, and handling fees.

Be wary of a *stalking horse bid*, where prior to the event, the auction house will select an entity from the pool of bidders to make the opening low-end bid to set the *reservation* or *floor price*. The entity making the bid is known as the *stalking horse*, which is derived from a hunter hiding behind a horse when pursuing a prey. Being the stalking horse bidder has some disadvantages and advantages. They accept the risk of setting the first bid as they may be stuck with the asset if others do not make a higher bid. In return, they gain the early insights on the asset and their due diligence costs are commonly reimbursed.

Blind Auction (aka First Price Sealed Bid)

Bidders place their offer in a sealed envelope and submit simultaneously to the auctioneer. The highest price is declared the winner. Bidders must have a thorough understanding of the assets, the process, fees/penalties, and key dates. The longest part of the preparation process is your evaluation of asset's value and securing your funding. Setting your profit margin target before the process begins will avoid bidding irrationally. To determine the optimal strategy, conduct in-depth research on the auction house, auctioneer and competition's bidding history and their current bidding resources.

Vickery Auction (aka Second Price Sealed Bid)

Bidders place their offer in a sealed envelope and simultaneously hand to the auctioneer with the highest price declared the winner, but only pays the second highest price. This process motivates bidders to offer a bid at or above the asset's market value as they assume the second price will be lower than their winning bid. Be aware of any seller participating with a shill bid to drive a higher price. This type of auction is vulnerable to bidder collusion.

Dutch Auction Bid (aka Open Descending Bid)

The auctioneer sets a relatively high price to the value of the asset and subsequently lowers the asking price in small increments until someone accepts the price, or the reservation price has been reached, thereby ending the process. The process is relatively fast and frequently used for initial public offerings (IPOs) and perishable commodities such as fish, flowers, and produce.

Two-Party Integrative Negotiation

Sometimes called *win–win* or *collective bargaining*. The strategy is structured to create a greater value with everyone benefiting from the upside. Participants understand the process must *grow the pie*, meaning everyone agrees to work together to increase the perceived value of the assets or services. The beginning value of the deal is speculative as each side will have different evaluations. Successful integrative negotiations focus on collaboration with some compromise for the greater good. There is minimal competitive positioning. Collaboration heightens the need for shared data and information. Understanding the other side's information needs is a path to a productive discussion. How you share it depends on the productivity and trust of the relationship. However, the side with the better data will have a negotiation edge.

A distributive negotiation is sometimes elevated to integrative when one side doesn't want to pay the market price and the other side has flexibility recognizing the value of other assets, services, or terms not in the original agreement. These have the potential for trade-offs to *grow the pie*.

The integrative strategy is to focus on collaboration, shared interests, creating value, problem-solving, and not positions, people, or market share grab. New variables are introduced to the negotiations to add value to the proposition. A common integrative negotiation strategy is to offer a lot of value options in the beginning to give the impression that you are collaborating at a high level. Some of these options may not have much value to others. A best practice is to keep a running tabulation of all alternatives to facilitate a fact-based discussion when the negotiation hits an impasse. Having a quantified *gives* list will help you leverage more toward the end.

There are two techniques to improve the integrative negotiation when you hit an impasse. The first is to give up something of value in the present to get more value later. The second is to trade something of hard value (e.g., revenue, costs) for soft value (e.g., service, quality). Letting the other side believe they have received something of greater value will be productive. Labor contracts and trade alliances are common examples of integrative negotiations.

Multiparty Integrative Negotiation

Integrative is best for multiple-party negotiations. One of the more difficult negotiations is when you have multiple parties and each believe they have an equal or greater say in the negotiation. When all parties insist on being represented at the negotiation table, the discussions will be lengthy and difficult.

The best multiparty strategy is to attain leadership of the negotiation by setting the meetings' time/place and controlling the agenda. Have the meetings at your office and strive to become the center of communication. This enables you to get all agreements and disagreements at one time so that no single party can leverage absences or delays. An added benefit for being the hub is the ability to form confidential alliances. Once you know the needs and wants of each party, you can parse the information on an *as-needed basis*. You have the best information and data to quantify the value of all available terms and be the clearinghouse for trade-offs.

Strive to gain majority support among the parties so that you can leverage the progress in your favor. Establishing the perception of creating a win–win in each situation prevents you from being left out. If you cannot lead, it is beneficial to insist on having a neutral outside entity manage the negotiation process.

Founder/Owner-Driven Negotiation

Founders/owners and celebrity CEOs have achieved their status believing they have a special set of skills that make them better at what they do than others. They can be narcissist, overconfident, and condescending in a negotiation. Know their skills and assets, such as technology, and prevent them from utilizing it to make you feel inferior. Negotiating with founders, owners, or high-profile CEOs takes more self-discipline and a willingness to experience unusual or disruptive behavior. When you decide the engagement is worth the challenge, then you must adapt your expectations and approach to the negotiation. You cannot expect them to change their attitude or behavior. Failure to adapt will cause frustration and indecisiveness.

The founder/owner can be led through a successful negotiation by knowing their influences and desire for success. Do extensive personal research on them as their behavior permeates the entire organization. Find out what motivates them and manipulate their strengths and vulnerabilities. Board of directors seats, favorite charities, and children's interests tend to be leverageable areas.

Insist on face-to-face meetings as your social and people skills are an advantage. Don't let them use their staff as interference. They will attend in person if they are interested in the deal. If they do not attend, you are likely a stalking horse.

The founder/owner sometimes start the meeting by mentioning their superior relationship with the someone in your circle of influence. This may look like an attempt at bonding, but it is their way to establish a superior position. Don't let them gain the edge by using a relationship with someone who can impact your career. Know these relationships before you engage so that you can deflect the potential impact. Confidentially solicit outside peers for references and support. Respond by how you are aligned in operating philosophies through your product, services, and charities.

To further enhance your integrity and trustworthiness, address everyone's concerns in the room no matter what their level in the organization. How you treat the lowest level employee on the other side will be a positive reflection on you. Respond enthusiastically to the lowest level person's comments. The advantage of propping-up the confidence of junior executives is they tend to overshare information inside and outside of the negotiation.

CHAPTER 8

The Negotiation Performance

How to Conduct the Three-Act Narrative

Every negotiation has its unique characters, settings, and plots. However, what is consistent is the negotiation narrative structure. Understanding the three acts of a negotiation will help achieve your goal and objective. Here are the negotiation plot points and how to gain the negotiation edge.

Act One—Part 1: Win the Initial Meeting

The two most important meetings of the negotiation are the first and closing meetings. Getting the initial meeting on your grounds gives you early control of the negotiation. Sports odds-makers give an advantage to the home team because teams perform better at home. Having the negotiation at your location gives you the edge.

If the other party insists on a neutral site, pick one where you have been before and have a relationship with the location's staff. A familiar environment gives you get better control of the meeting. A nice setting with known resources and a responsive service staff gives you the edge.

Hosting the First Meeting: Advantages

Having the first meeting on your grounds improves your focus, reduces complexity, and avoids distractions. Hosting requires additional prep work, but it is better than having to manage unfamiliar location, directions, late arrivals, parking, security, restrooms, Wi-Fi, projectors, screens, bringing the right materials, and seating arrangements. The visiting side has a longer day, especially when personal time is used to travel. The home team focus is entirely on the meeting performance and results.

Another benefit of hosting the first negotiation meeting is the opportunity to create an environment so that the other side will feel good about working with you. Although both sides participate in setting the meeting's start time and length, it is the host who controls the atmosphere of the meeting. Like a dinner party, it is the host's responsibility to make the visitors feel comfortable and have an enjoyable and productive experience. A comfortable environment creates a higher probability of making progress. When the other side is relaxed, you have the edge.

Being a good host is beneficial even if the meeting is not going well. If the host has provided a pleasant environment, it will be harder to end the discussions. It is easier to abruptly end an unproductive meeting when the conditions are poor.

Hosting the First Meeting: Disadvantages

The disadvantage of hosting is the difficulty to go *nuclear* and end the meeting abruptly. Physically leaving the meeting before the agenda is achieved is a forceful communication. If the traveling party is unhappy with the direction of the meeting, they can simply get up and walk away. The host cannot abruptly walk out of a meeting. A party host cannot announce, "I don't like the conversation. Good night, everyone!"

The host is responsible for the productive tone and pacing of the negotiation. The visiting side can take the position of *make me happy*. The host needs to read the other side to ensure the meeting is going well. If the other side is getting antsy, the tone and pacing need to change to keep engagement at a high level.

Gain the Edge by Owning the Agenda

Another advantage of hosting the first meeting is the assumptive right to provide the written agenda. The agenda controls the discussion and initially puts the home team on the offensive. Owning the agenda allows the lead negotiator to develop the script that sets the direction of the negotiation. A well-written agenda can extract key information from the other side. The visiting team is immediately put on the defensive by having to react to the agenda. The agenda issues will be directed to the other leader, but sometimes can be written as open questions for anyone on the other side. Encouraging members on the other side to talk is advantageous. Someone may try to prove how smart they are by revealing critical information.

When controlling the agenda, have one of your staff keep track of time to ensure you get the key discussion topics covered within a reasonable time. You need to allow time for agenda creep or tangential topics, which will extend discussions. Plan breaks for every two hours. Don't be overly ambitious by trying to squeeze too much into the initial meeting.

Gain the Edge by Papering the Deal

Writing the meeting agenda gives you the opening to physically write the contract drafts and final agreement. The attorneys on both sides will want to have this responsibility as it allows one side to shape the interpretation of each term to their liking. Getting agreement on the exact wording of every term is difficult and time consuming. Don't wait until the end of the negotiation to fight over the nuances of the wording. Focus on the exact wording throughout the negotiation. If left until the very end, one side may try to leverage any word changes to their advantage.

Gain the Edge by Writing the Follow-Up Meeting Notes

The host of the initial meeting and owner of the agenda should provide the follow-up written meeting notes within 24 hours of the meeting. These are to be sent by the lead negotiator to all attendees with a *confidential* label on a secured digital platform. The content of the follow-up notes should include what was agreed to, what is outstanding, who will perform follow-up tasks along with the time and place of the next meeting. Written notes are better communication for accuracy and timelines. Writing and distributing the follow-up notes will establish your fairness, trustworthiness, and credibility. No new terms, additional thoughts, or subjective commentary should be in the notes. You cannot change anyone's POV in follow-up notes. The goal is a shared understanding and one version of the truth in the briefest memo possible.

Follow-up phone calls can be helpful to explain a complex follow-up note, but don't use it to confirm or deny a discussion point. That is best done in the follow-up meeting. Only the lead negotiator should be making or receiving phone calls about the negotiation. Be aware when someone from the other negotiation team calls someone on your team. No one from your team should be communicating to the other side at any time during the negotiation.

Act One—Part 2: The Dance of the First Offer

Each side begins the negotiations with an overly optimistic view the deal will get done. However, both parties may be hesitant to make the first offer. Getting the other side to make the first move is the *dance of the first offer*. One side needs to subtly take the lead like in ballroom dancing. Both are engaged, circling, and getting comfortable until one feels ready to execute a well-coordinated dip—the first offer. Sometimes it is being the first to request the other party to *send me the paperwork*. This usually happens with short-term or renewal agreements having templated contracts with only minimal changes permitted. Examples are auto purchases and retail vendor agreements. Having to make the first offer has disadvantages for both the seller and buyer.

Seller Making the Initial Offer—Disadvantages

- The price will never get higher.
- Seller's remorse: If immediately accepted, did you price too low?
- Often rejected due to assumption that there will eventually be a lower price.
- If too high, it runs the risk of the other party walking away or seeking a competitor's offer.

Buyer Making the Initial Offer—Disadvantages

- The price will never be lower.
- Buyer's remorse: If accepted, did I pay too much?

- Rarely accepted unless well above market price.
- Seller will decide on your potential of doing a deal with others and react accordingly.

How to Make the Initial Offer

A long-term, customized agreement in an emerging market has more inherent risk for both sides. This makes it harder to get one party to make the first offer. If you must make the first offer, try to avoid giving a specific price or value. Present the big picture and how a fair deal will be good for the total business or the industry in which you both participate. Discuss your company's position in the market and scale the opportunities for both parties. Try to gain a consensus with your outlook of the market-place and its impact on both companies. Identify how you perceive the other party's role in the category or market. Gain the edge by making the other side respond to your perception of the market. This is the first indication how your offer will be received.

If an existing deal is expiring, focus on the why the deal does not work for you and the rationale for changes. Provide support on how you adjusted the terms to account for emerging opportunities or threats. Effectively communicate your *needs* and *wants*. Gain the edge by including some fake *needs* and *wants* so that you can trade them out later in the process.

If you must give a price, present it in person with nothing in writing. This will enable you to read the other leader's reaction and minimize it being shopped to competitors. Avoid giving a range as it will become the *reservation price*. If your price is outright rejected, take the high road by calmly stating all other terms and items to be considered for the deal. Don't compete against yourself by adjusting your initial offer. Wait for their counteroffer.

How to Respond to the Initial Offer

The second most important action in a negotiation is the response to the initial offer. It takes you on a course that is difficult to change. Think carefully what you want to communicate. Appear calm and rational while actively listening. Ask questions on everything you do not understand.

Do not assume anything. Getting clarification can give you the edge by potentially getting an early *give* and avoiding unfavorable surprises at the end of the negotiation.

Do not give a positive or negative indication to any of your responses. Stay emotionally disciplined because nonverbal reactions can reveal your true interest. If you are too aggressive or unrealistic, the other side may immediately walk away because they think that you are not a serious partner. Some negotiators like to open with an extreme offer expecting the other side will counter with a reasonable offer with an expectation of compromise at a *skewed midpoint*. However, extreme initial offers create the potential for multiple unproductive rounds before realistic progress is made.

Take a measured approach to a complex offer by breaking down the deal terms into manageable parts. Label and prioritize each part by monetary value and anticipated difficulty in resolving. Compare the list to the total value of the deal to keep the importance of each individual parts in perspective. Then, add qualitative pluses and minuses of each term. Do any of these subjective values have an impact on the monetary value of the terms? These could include company image, industry standing, and political or environmental impacts.

Offer Response Strategy: Easy First

Once you have evaluated the proposal, choose between two response strategies: *Easy first* or *hard first*. Easy first focuses on the agreeable terms. This creates momentum of the *sequential yes* psychological factor. Getting each side to say *yes* to a string of terms creates a positive psychological effect. Everyone feels good about the early progress and becomes optimistic before addressing the more difficult topics. It is best to use this response strategy in large meetings with many attendees. The easy first strategy eliminates the potential for one party to become frustrated from the lack of progress, force a defensive posture, or walk away.

The disadvantage using the easy first response strategy is that it can cause problems later in the negotiation. Previous points of agreement are not available to trade for unresolved items of equal value later in the negotiations. Another downside is when one side feels they have given too much and want to revise a previous agreed-to term. These two *claw back* situations may inhibit momentum, reduce progress, and cause frustration.

Offer Response Strategy: Hard First

Hard first is the second response strategy where the most difficult terms are addressed initially. Each side responds by providing their rationale why these terms cannot be accepted. This provides ample time to discuss and resolve the harder issues. Both sides have fresh perspectives and the energy to devote to a resolution. Hard first works best with the leaders negotiating one-on-one or in small groups. Larger meetings have difficulty with the hard first strategy due to the multiple sources of negative commentary creating widespread pessimism and a lack of progress.

Your initial response, either easy first or hard first does not to have to be in writing as you may need to acquiesce later. Gain an edge by starting with a conservative reaction on the size of each gap and the conditions that need to be met to accept each term. Position the response as a *feeler* and not a counteroffer to minimize the risk of an abrupt ending to the negotiation. Do not let the other side believe the gap is so wide that negotiating is a waste of time. Your tone needs to be sincere and credible without any bluster or posturing. The party that walks away will be perceived as the rationale side, and you will be accused of being unreasonable. Always keep the other party engaged by assuming the high ground with the phrases "what is best for the industry," "what is best for both companies," and "what is best for our shared customer." Sometimes, negotiations are a one-act play and completed after the response to the first offer. However, most times the negotiation's outcome is highly dependent resolving difficult issues in the second act.

Act Two—Part 1: Hitting the First Impasse

After multiple meetings and counteroffers, each side's position will become apparent. The pace and tone of the exchanges will reveal the likelihood of completing a deal. Be aware of any dramatic changes in the other side's behavior. Have they stated their positions irrationally or vented their emotions on key issues? A common overreaction is when a negative response exceeds the issue's importance to the overall deal. Another is a broad hyperbolic negative statement such as, "that will kill our profitability" or "that is way above the market." Overreactions and irrational positions are *negotiation smoke detectors* that signal an impasse will occur.

When progress has stalled, take a break and decompress. A few days of silence can be good for both sides to refocus on the priorities and solutions. Recalibrate your communication strategy how you want to react to the other side. Take the time to get more information and a different perspective. Revisit all the analytics to ensure you are seeing the assumptions and alternatives clearly. Break issues down into the smallest manageable parts and solve them one at a time.

You need to be mentally strong and emotionally resilient during the first impasse of a negotiation. Try to mitigate any irrational escalations. Your biggest obstacle can be your own emotions. You cannot control your counterpart's behavior, only *how you react to that behavior*. Demonstrate respect and strive to maintain integrity and trust. Whichever side gets angry first is an indication who has the most to lose either personally or professionally. Finding the underlying motivation for their anger will uncover their vulnerability. Don't call them out on their *weaknesses*. Keep your gunpowder dry until poking that weakness will get a bigger reward near the end. It is too early to go nuclear by walking away or getting the other side's leader removed. There will be a time toward the end of the negotiation to consider those moves.

Positive emotions lead to generosity and helpfulness. Keep it friendly with affirmations and compliments. Do not try to use humor to diffuse the situation. Sarcasm exposes your negative feelings and may create animosity. It only takes one misinterpreted joke to create tension in the room. Putting your opponent on the defensive or causing frustration will make the negotiation more difficult. Keep it friendly as possible—even if you must fake it. Tension reduces trust. Try to position the deal as the *common enemy* and not your counterpart.

Determine who on the other side is rational and partially agrees with you. Reach out to them through a shared relationship to establish some common ground on the difficult issues. Don't expect insubordination, but finding a rational counterpart is a useful asset. It is best to establish this relationship before the negotiation.

Act Two—Part 2: Solving the First Impasse

Is It Us?

The first step to solve the impasse is to conduct a thorough self-examination. Ask yourself tough questions. A good leader will provide an honest evaluation that will create the next plan of action. Try to see the deal objectively from their side. What is preventing your side from making progress toward an agreement? Are there any new facts or data that may necessitate adjusting your goal, objective, or strategies? Is your communication to the other side productive? Are you overconfident or have an unreasonable position? Hiring an outside consultant can give a fresh perspective. An objective third party can be effective identifying and resolving personality or communication issues. Fresh eyes and unbiased minds can help get to a mutually satisfactory place.

Is It Them?

Analyze why the other side is not being productive. Do you know their organization and business well enough to understand their position? Is there a mutual commitment to reach an agreement? Are expectations at the same level? Have they surprised you with anything? If your counterpart is angry or disappointed, it may be due to disrespect, deception, unfairness, humiliation, or loss of pride. You cannot dismiss their feelings, even though they may not be justified by you. Revisit these pain points, acknowledge their presence, and express empathy for these feelings. Keep the negotiation about issues and not personalities. A negotiation leader needs to have business maturity and a high emotional IQ to resolve an impasse.

Are the Differences Irreconcilable?

Identify all the specific unresolved issues and the root cause for the impasse. Are the quantitative (monetary) and qualitative (feelings) values consistent on both sides? Analyze the contradictory data. Does either side have unrealistic expectations? Are risk and reward outcomes aligned? Does either side need more downside protection or bigger share of the upside? Now is the time to give up your fake *needs* and *wants* to soften the other side's position.

An effective immediate solution to an impasse is to suggest a shorter deal length to minimize variabilities and reduce the risk. A shorter time period should make both sides' projections more accurate. Each side will have more confidence and need fewer safeguards. You can implement targets that will trigger a new negotiation if conditions or performance exceed these guardrails.

There may be some resistance to shortening the deal length because of human nature. Less experienced negotiation leaders tend to avoid another grueling engagement for as long as possible. This is especially true when there are multiple deals to negotiate around the same time.

Is one side stalling to allow time to recalibrate strategies or pursue a competing offer? A method to intentionally slow the negotiation is to offer a package of complex options. This forces the other side to request more time to analyze the options. This delay tactic does have risk as the other side may get frustrated and walk away from the negotiation.

When it is time to re-engage the other side, start out with a statement of good intentions and why the deal still makes sense for all involved. Highlight your progress and all the commonalities both parties have. Convince them to be optimistic based on either new information, a new position on key issues, or changes in the market conditions. Now it is time to sell them!

Act Three—Part 1: A Surprise Emerges

When you have solved the initial impasse, your supervisor and stakeholders will believe a deal is imminent. Avoid this mindset and never state you think a deal will get done. You hope the deal will happen; you just don't know at this time. The recommended response to the status question is "I am cautiously optimistic about the deal." The negotiation gap from the updated battlefield map can provide a quantitative response such as, "we are $1 million dollars apart on a $50 million deal value." Any public optimism on your side may create vulnerability the other side may try to leverage.

Coming out of the first impasse, one side may believe an agreement will happen more than the other. This is a highly leverageable situation where two challenges can emerge. The first is a new onerous deal term is presented. The second is a new authority injects themselves into the negotiation process.

When either situation happens, the leader needs to inform the organization's management. Do not keep it quiet or expect it to be resolved quickly. The leader–supervisor discussion typically begins with the phrase, "I need to make your aware of…." Always communicate bad news in person so that you can read the true reaction from your supervisor. This will increase your supervisor's sense of responsibility. They will be compelled to acknowledge the difficulty of the situation and offer encouragement with suggested solutions. You will be asked for your recommendation on how to proceed. Be prepared and confident with your recommendation. Any uncertainty will encourage your supervisor to push you aside and inject themselves directly into the proceedings. The supervisor will then get the credit for closing the good deal or killing the bad deal you supported. Either outcome is bad for your reputation and career.

Surprise #1: The Late, Onerous Proposal

When a completely new adverse deal term is proposed by the other side, it could cause a second impasse. Your initial reaction is to call *foul*. This is a negotiation, not a game, and there is no referee. A good leader should be able to minimize the difficulty and resolve it. Your team may fracture at this point. Some team members may want to walk away from the deal. Others may want to give in just to get the deal done. They may say, "We have worked too long and hard not to get this done." Ignore them. Keep everyone focused on the company goal and negotiation objective.

Take the necessary time to analyze the impact and determine the optimal reaction. A delayed response will make the other side feel less confident. Find the source of this new term by asking open-ended questions. If you find the source, you will find the solution. There are two viable response options. First, accept their change to get a firm commitment to close the deal now. If you do this, immediately make changes to the written contract and have them sign it first. There is no flexibility, compromises, or favors. If you do not stand firm accepting no more changes, you will lose the negotiation edge to close this deal favorably.

The second response option is to get something of equal or slightly greater value added in return. Resist the temptation to overreact by striking back harder with something of far greater value. Utilize a collaborative trade-off strategy by getting something in return *in the future* such as more of the upside or better protection on the downside. Make sure anything you ask for is tangible and measurable so that there is no misunderstanding in the interpretation of the term. Avoid such phrasing as *best efforts* and *market standard* as these are hard to enforce. Your *get-in-return* should be written to withstand scrutiny in a court of law.

The second viable trade-off is getting *schmuck insurance*, a safety clause used to mitigate a deal turning unfavorable to you or highly favorable to the other side due to unforeseen circumstances. This insurance term must contain tangible and measurable terminology, which requires in-depth industry knowledge to get right. The protection would be triggered when the deal reaches a threshold and becomes *significantly* unfavorable to you or *overly* favorable for the other side. The first situation is getting relief you cannot reach performance targets such as a profit level. The second situation ensures better participation in the upside from a tremendous windfall for the other side.

Schmuck insurance is a *good give* for both parties to use at the very end of a negotiation. Good schmuck insurance requires compliance and transparency with firm dates, prices, and service-level commitments. Consider hiring a third party with industry experience to develop schmuck insurance for your agreement.

Surprise #2: The Leader Change

There are many reasons why a new leader emerges late in the process. Usually, it is the lack of progress and/or an imminent deadline. When a new leader or decision maker appears, it tends to be a Hammer. They enter with strong support from the highest levels in the organization and are not interested in the details or how the impasse occurred. They want results and will demand an immediate compromise to close the deal. Do not give up anything in the initial Hammer meeting. Listen to the rants without reacting.

A Hammer's weakness is impatience and details. Use an effective stall tactic initially if you are not vulnerable to an immediate deadline. Extend the process by being methodical and objective. Try to regain control by slowly leading the Hammer through the rank order of your needs and wants. State your points firmly and calmly. Any weakness in your position will fuel their energy to squeeze you. The best defensive tactic is getting the Hammer to believe you have an equally good or better alternative to this deal.

Another defensive tactic is to engage external stakeholders to believe the Hammer is blowing up a mutually beneficial deal. Hammers' egos can be influenced by outside opinions. Their public reputation is important to them. Your publicity person or an industry veteran are good sources who can attack the Hammer from the outside. Hammers will listen to a credible source if told to "lighten up," "don't blow this deal," or "pull it back a notch." The more professional downside you can create for the Hammer, the easier it will be to have productive discussions.

In the end, sometimes life is too short to engage the Hammer's difficult persona. Nothing good comes from any irrational escalation of the terms. Keep your ego in check. Rely on the numbers and not the subjective factors. Don't drift outside your objective or performance targets. Avoid attempts to improve the deal's outlook with soft items such as *synergy savings*. Refer to your preparation's hard and soft costs. Identify and avoid stakeholders who are personally incentivized to get the deal done, such as investment bankers and business development executives. Credible explanations for walking away are "Not the right time for this deal" and "There is too much volatility in market."

Act Three—Part 2: The Second Impasse Solution

The last effort to save a negotiation is to get the top person on each side to meet at a neutral site. The two questions for the discussion are "Is this deal, in its many versions, good for both of us?" and "Can we work together once there is an agreement?" Expect to hear both compromises and walk-away threats in the discussion. One side may need more time, and another may want to close the deal now. Do not try to *will the close of the deal* at this time. The conversations should be calm and thoughtful. The person who offers the most positive rationale is the one who wants the deal to close. Let the other side do most of the talking. This is where your reputation as a negotiator is made.

By this time, an experienced negotiation leader will know whether to do the deal. Walking away to avoid an overly expensive deal can give your organization the opportunity to shift strategy, get better execution on current business, and potentially generate better results. Your negotiation reputation will be determined by your behavior. It is the only thing the other side and stakeholders will remember. The ultimate results of the deal will only be remembered by two people: yourself and your supervisor.

The Soft Close: I Think We Have a Deal

In new romantic relationships, it is awkward to be the first one to say, "I love you." A negotiated deal operates under the same premise. When the last deal point is done, *do not* be the first one to announce, "I think we have a deal." Whoever says it first indicates they need the deal more than the other side. It is socially difficult *not to respond* when a handshake is offered to close a deal. To gain the edge, your reaction should be, "The situation is very positive, but do we have a deal?" This will encourage them to recap all the high points and the rationale for a deal. Now you can gain the final negotiation edge by making a *nibble*: a last request to add or change a term.

If you are being nibbled, react with one of equal or greater size and importance. Once the other side knows that you will counter hard with any last-minute nibbling, the one-upmanship will end. At this point, each side is looking for equilibrium and assurances everything is a go. Neither side wants the annoyance of having to give up something after the handshake.

A surprising number of deals fall apart after the handshake because leaders do not know how to close a deal. It is like climbing a mountain; once you reached the summit, you must maintain focus to safely descend. Most climbing accidents happen on the way down. Cleaning up loose ends should happen before the close.

Gain the Edge by Papering the Final Draft—Now!

As the leader, you must remain disciplined and diligent to prevent an unexpected derailing. Distributing the written agreement to both parties in less than 24 hours after the final meeting will minimize lapses in memory, internal second guessing, and nibbles. Don't accept the suggestion to wait until the end of the negotiation to begin to draft the final agreement. The attorney drafting the deal should have been updating the latest draft after each meeting. Both side's approvers should have been prepped on the deal status *before* the final negotiation meeting. Getting their final approval will need to be a quick meeting.

Act Three—Part 3: Hard Close and Celebration

The last negotiation meeting has both sides simultaneously reviewing the final written agreement with all attachments. Each leader needs to make themselves available for questions and immediate resolutions. Gather your team in a war room and meticulously review every letter and comma. Do not rush or skip any pages, including any exhibits. Does your interpretation of the contract wording have an ambiguities? Does it meet your expectations exactly? Put yourself in the mindset that you are defending this document in a lawsuit.

Get the Written Agreement Signed

Once you are satisfied with the document and the pages are locked, it needs the approver's signature. It is best to have one source sending out the documents to the approvers to avoid any confusion or mismatched documents. The drafting attorney is responsible to get the document to each approver in a timely and confidential manner. The most efficient method is to send the documents electronically with encryption from a secured platform.

Each approver, if not the negotiation leader, should be very familiar with the contents of the document as they should have been kept informed along the way. However, there are occasions where an authority wants to prove their status, intelligence, or toughness by taking more time than necessary to approve a written contract. As the leader, you need to do whatever it takes to get the authorized signature as quickly as possible.

Leaks in confidentiality peak between the time of the handshake and signed document. Sometimes the strength of your relationship with your negotiation team and stakeholders isn't enough to prevent leaks. Particpants get very excited and want to convey the news of an agreement to their work and social circles. When critical information gets out too early, it can undermine your position and threaten the deal. If confidentiality is being compromised, create uncertainty and confusion with those suspected of leaking. Give them various *misdirection information* to contrast the leaked information. Your publicity and sales executives are adept at disseminating camouflage news.

Make the Simultaneous Announcement

Another way to reduce confidentiality leaks is to coordinate the publicity release before the deal signing. While the attorneys are working on the contract, both side's publicity staff should be cowriting a general release statement. Key information is codeveloped along with optimistic quotes from the leaders of the negotiation and their organizations. Both sides need to be involved in the writing and approval of the final draft. Although the release will be coauthored, it is best to have one source writing the release, and the other approving.

The Celebration

You should feel a sense of accomplishment when the deal is signed. Completing a negotiation is an achievement that should be recognized and celebrated. Keep the celebration small and personal to avoid criticism from jealous peers and colleagues. Invite your immediate supervisor and the people who contributed to the negotiation. Any visible celebration has the potential to bring out a negative reaction from stakeholders or coworkers who resent your success and admonish the celebration as wasteful and undeserved. The workplace is a competitive environment. It only takes one person to start a disparaging campaign with some aspect of the negotiation.

After signing the deal, the first inclination is to vent your suppressed emotions by expressing how difficult the negotiation was and how the other side did not behave well. Broadly communicating the difficulty of the process will open you up to criticism from others who "could have done it better." Be humble and appreciative of everyone who worked on the deal. Publicly display good sportsmanship by praising the other side for being worthy negotiators throughout the negotiation. A good postnegotiation comment for colleagues is "They were really good negotiators. The results show we got the best deal possible."

The Debriefing

The final step is to ensure the deal will be executed at the highest levels by those who are accountable in your organization. The leader and members of the negotiation team usually have some accountability; however, there are others who may share responsibility. While discussions with these people should have occurred throughout the negotiation, now is the time to disseminate complete information about the deal to get their full commitment.

As soon as the deal is signed, meet with those responsible for the execution to communicate the key performance metrics and incentives. Let them know upfront the deal cannot be changed, but listen when they offer better opportunities or vent their challenges. These should not be a surprise, so prepare appropriate responses. Do not be dismissive to the negative comments. Encourage collaboration by letting others in the room offer their solutions first. Arrive at a consensus on how these issues will be managed. Your goal is to prevent anyone from leaving the room thinking they cannot execute the deal. Failure to get commitment on the execution will make the deal vulnerable to underperformance.

Set a plan to have regular updates on the performance of the deal with those responsible. Create a one-page summary of the key success metrics and track the performance. The scorecard should be reviewed by management on predetermined intervals such as quarterly and annually. The document will be comanaged by personnel other than the negotiating team to ensure transparency and compliance. Strategic planning or finance departments are best suited for this task.

The Aftermath: Performance Review

There is one more important follow-up to ensure this and subsequent negotiations are successful. It is a good business practice to conduct two negotiation performance reviews: one on the total process and the other on the leader's performance. The negotiation process review is an objective scorecard providing historical context and continuity for any subsequent deals. There are three parts to the review: engagement, negotiating process, and results. The leader's performance review is an opportunity for the supervisor, peers, and staff to critique the performance and guide future negotiation behavior. The best way to improve negotiation performance is to identify key actions and measure them to ensure success on the next negotiation.

Overall Performance

- Value: What is the value of the deal, and how does it contribute to the future success of the organization?
- Interests: Did the deal address stakeholder interests and concerns?
- Projections: Accurate and completed in a timely manner?
- Options: Were options considered to completing the deal and presented internally? What was the best alternative to making the deal?
- Legitimacy: Did the offer presented and received by the other side meet or exceed industry standards?
- Relationship: Does the other side feel good about the agreement? Has a productive working relationship between the two organizations been established?

Leadership Performance

- Objectives: Negotiation results were aligned to the organization's objectives?
- Preparation: Team's roles and responsibilities clearly identified?
- Flexibility: The key learnings from the meetings adjusted deal terms accordingly?
- Rational Thinking: Ability to see both sides to the deal?
- Problem-Solving: Identified barriers to a deal and provided solutions?

- Communication: Stakeholders and the decision maker received relevant information?
- Formed productive coalitions and addressed the unproductive coalitions effectively?
- Exhibited integrity and established trust?
- Organization is committed to making the deal work?

Company XYZ Negotiation Team Performance Evaluation Example					
Item	Description	Evaluator's Comments	Importance Factor to the Negotiation (0.0–1.0)	Score (1–5)	Grade (1.0–5.00)
Decision to Engage	Preparation and Decision Process		High (1.0)	5	5.00
Value #1	Achieved Company Goal		High (1.0)	4	4.00
Value #2	Achieved Company Objective		High (1.0)	4	4.00
Preparation	Quantity and Quality		High (1.0)	4	4.00
Strategies	Effectiveness of Strategies		High (1.0)	4	4.00
Alternative Course of Action	Developed and Evaluated Potential Alternatives		Medium (0.75)	4	3.00
Negotiation Behavior	Professional and Productive		Medium (0.75)	3	2.25
Negotiation Timing	Productive Pace and Executed Before Deadline		Low (0.50)	4	2.00
Negotiation-Teamwork	Lead Team to a Successful Conclusion		Low (0.50)	5	2.50
Other	Additional Thoughts		Low (0.50)	3	1.50
Total Score	Out of Possible 40				30.75

Figure 8.1 Negotiation performance evaluation example

CHAPTER 9

Negotiating Content Deals

Matching Risk and Reward

There are *five essential elements* in every content negotiation: Defining the content specifications, documenting ownership, estimating the concept value, understanding the creator/owner's motivations, and determining the optimal deal structure. The best deal structure is a complex equation balancing reward with risk in an evolving entertainment market.

Defining the Content Specifications

The first step is knowing the exact *specifications of the asset*, which includes identifying the current stage of development. Content description must be written into the agreement with specific details. There can be no assumptions or vagueness about the asset.

Negotiating for creative assets is challenging because everyone has a different perception of the content's value. The path from script to screen rarely achieves the same expectations of the creator, owner, or buyer. Getting a consensus on an asset's expected *level of quality* is difficult. Legal language defines quality in contracts as *industry standards* and *best efforts to create*.... These are difficult to enforce. Negotiations tend to be easier when all parties have similar expectations.

The need for *quality protection* in a deal is heightened when there are multiple movies or TV episodes/seasons. Buyers can protect themselves with an *early exit clause* when the perceived quality is uncertain. This allows one party to avoid paying the full price if the content does not meet expectations. Stretching out the payment terms gives the buyer some leverage in disputes over quality. Common payment terms are

30 percent at the agreement signing, 30 percent commencing production, and 40 percent upon a satisfactory delivery of final product.

Documenting Ownership

The one content deal term where there can be no difference in perception or fact is the ownership rights to the intellectual property (IP). The first meeting should identify the IP owner and confirm with a 100 percent accurate *trail of ownership document.*

A common ownership problem in content agreements are *development or alteration rights.* Content agreements need to clarify rights to alter the underlying property. Understanding content alteration rights avoids making two big financial mistakes: buying into a money pit and not having the rights to release it. The buyer must know the property's stage of development, production schedule, and development costs needed to complete the project.

Another topic of ownership dispute is when there is a *material change* to the content. When a project in development has something significantly added, the change may trigger a previous rights issue. The past owner may have rights when the content is altered and greater potential is created. One aspect of the chain of ownership is to review previous option periods to ensure there has been a clearly defined termination or transfer clause.

Even the big studios can fail to confirm ownership rights. Warner Bros. and Fox had a dispute with *The Watchmen* movie rights. The original graphic novel was created in 1987 for DC Comics, a division of Warner Bros. Fox Studio and producer Larry Gordon bought/optioned the movie rights and over the next few years tried in vain to get the movie made. By 2007, Warner Bros. believed the movie rights expired and reverted to them.

Historically, studio contracts were typed on paper, placed in file cabinets, and eventually sent to a long-term storage facility. Executives move, offices change, and files are lost. Prior to 2007, it was not uncommon to have portions of IP contracts lost when there was a change of business affairs personnel. It's one of the reasons studios were reluctant to change their top business affairs executives. Now content agreements are stored on digital files and easily accessed to avoid what happened with *THE WATCHMEN.*

Warner Bros. and Legendary Pictures spent over U.S.$100 million to produce *THE WATCHMEN* film in 2008. Right before the film was to be released to theaters, Fox filed a lawsuit and won an injunction to stop the exhibition of the movie. The court ruled Fox owned the movie rights. This ruling enabled Fox to negotiate a favorable settlement from Warner Bros. to distribute the film.

Estimating the Content's Value

The foundation of any content negotiation is the content's potential commercial value. All parties in the negotiation will develop their own revenue projections, called an *ultimate*. The ability to accurately estimate the content's future revenue creates a negotiation edge in the negotiation preparation. Studios and digital platforms have developed sophisticated forecasting models built from comparative lists or *comps*. These content assets having similar performance metrics: market trends, geography, revenue, genre, talent, budget, release dates, and target audience.

Studio forecasting models can accurately project a movie or TV show's lifetime revenue, after just one week of performance in the market. Entertainment viewership is surprisingly consistent worldwide with a few genre exceptions. Franchise and action films are highly predictable, while comedy and dramas are more nuanced. Another variable is projecting revenues for international territories as local markets tastes vary with lesser genres. The term for this situation is how well does *a property travel.*

Know the Creator/Owner's Motivation

Knowing the creator/owner's motivation and priorities provide a negotiation edge. These motivations can be segmented into three categories of psychological needs: for *attention*, to express a *personal message*, and to support a *desired lifestyle*. The most effective way to learn the creator's true motivation is to socialize with them. They will reveal their intentions in a comfortable setting better than an office. It is best not to have their intermediaries (friend, agent, or attorney) present as they will likely obfuscate the creator's true needs. Intermediaries tend to inject their own interests into the deal.

Creating content is mentally and physically difficult. The creators live with the content for such a long time, they have difficulty being objective about the quality. They are like parents believing their baby (content) is beautiful with unlimited potential. This attitude makes creators highly sensitive to well-intentioned improvement suggestions. Any criticism can be viewed by the creator as not understanding their intent. Criticism must be well thought-out and offered cautiously with extreme sensitivity to the creator's feelings. A negotiation edge is created by convincing the creator that you will help the content reach its full potential or said another way—*finds its largest audience.*

Content Deal Structure Options

Deal structures are based on three functions: who *does* the work, who *approves* the work, and how *the proceeds are shared.* These activities are negotiated based on each party's talent, market knowledge, available resources, and level of risk. The two basic content deal structures are *distribution fee* and *royalty/revenue sharing.*

Distribution Fee

Also known as a *sales force for hire* deal. In this structure, the *content owner pays* a percentage of the contracted definition of the net revenue to the distributor for marketing, selling, and collecting proceeds from specified accounts, geography, and time period. Fees normally range between 10 and 20 percent. The content owner needs to have strong market knowledge as they approve all aspects of the project.

The definitions are important with two key terms in the contract: *net revenue or proceeds* and *length of the collection period.* Net revenue is defined by gross revenue less expenses such as distribution fee, preapproved discounts, credit terms, shipping and returns expenses, and placement fees. Most disputes arise when the owner is surprised by unexpected expenses deducted from the gross revenues. This can happen when *each* of the participants has *different* definitions of net revenue. The variations are a way of rewarding each participant differently. The distributor will defend each of the deductions as a cost of doing business and normal trade practices.

It is best to have the *expense deductions* discussion toward the end of the negotiation as this topic can go poorly quickly. The discussion will reveal how well the creator/owner knows the market and if the two parties can work together. Any distribution agreement, regardless of the level of trust, needs to be transparent with audit rights.

A distribution fee deal allows content owners to make all the creative and business decisions, including production, manufacturing, mastering, pricing, release dates, marketing, and inventory ownership. Determining the *price* and level of *marketing spending* are the owner's decisions with the biggest impact to in-market performance. The marketing spending level can be negotiated into the deal. Generally, content owners do not have the available cash to pay for a marketing campaign. The distributor will forward or *loan* the marketing funds, which will be deducted from the net revenue. This marketing advance puts risk onto the distributor who may go *unrecouped*, should the content underperform.

The other contested discussion point is setting the price. Content owners in a distribution fee structure need to have good knowledge of the industry to know the optimal price. Both parties need realistic expectations for consumer demand with respect for the content's price elasticity. Content creators tend to be overly optimistic and lean toward a higher price with minimal discounts and credit terms. An above-market price may limit the commercial potential by not reaching a wide audience. Should the project fail to meet expectations, creators tend to believe the consumer rejected the price, not the content.

The distributor will lean toward a lower price with more discounts and longer credit terms to help the sell-in and attract a wider audience. Pricing is critical for transactional entertainment models such as movie tickets, DVD, and transactional video-on-demand, while digital subscription models make it less critical.

Royalty Fee

Also known as *revenue sharing* deal. The *distributor pays* the content owner a percentage of the contracted definition of net revenue for control of the

IP. Fees usually range from 8 to 20 percent. The entity with the most risk gets the authority to make the critical decisions.

Once again, the net collected revenue or proceeds definition needs to be clearly written and understood by the content owner. In this model, the distributor is doing most of the work and getting most of the reward. The distributor is responsible for all the costs, including manufacturing, marketing, distribution, overhead expenses, and inventory ownership. The royalty fee is usually paid on a quarterly basis; however, there can be delays of up to 30 to 60 days due to the complex calculations of direct and indirect costs.

The royalty structure is preferred by content owners who do not have adequate knowledge of the marketplace nor the resources to maximize the project's potential. Owners need to trust the distributor will act in the best interest of the property. Distributors prefer the royalty structure when they are confident in the product and can control the property with minimal disruptive input from the owners.

The royalty structure enables the distributor to decide on the level of marketing. This expenditure is rarely communicated to the content owner as they think it's never enough. Creators believe the marketing spend level is an indication on the distributor's confidence in the content. In a competitive bidding situation, distributors may have to commit to a marketing level to close the deal.

The release date decision is solely decided by the distributors. Occasionally, the date is disputed by a creator who has little regard to the competitive market. Content owners can have unrealistic expectations believing their content will be everyone's first choice on the release date. Good distributors have the data to support their date, but occasionally, there are *contracted release dates* where the content owner has enough leverage to select the date in the agreement.

Content owners need to trust the distributor will make decisions in the best interest of the property; however, the expectations for amount of communication can be problematic. Content owners tend to expect the distributor to discuss everything with them. The distributor tend to provide information on an *as-needed* basis. Putting a *service-level agreement* (SLA) into the contract will ensure a productive working relationship. Royalty contracts use terms such as *meaningful discussions* or *consultation* when the owners want to have their opinions heard and don't fully trust the relationship.

Minimum Guarantee

Also known as the *MG* or *the advance*. It is the contracted upfront payment for either a distribution or royalty structured deal. The payment timing can be in lump sum or multiple payments prior to the release to the market. The buyer recoups from the money collected until the advance is paid back or recouped.

Content owners often look at the minimum guarantee to determine how much a distributor likes the property and the level of confidence in the product. The amount is usually a percentage (e.g., 50 percent) of the expected total value of the agreement.

Top distributors can pay below-market minimum guarantees by leveraging their position in the market, resources, and unique abilities. Content owners benefit from having a distributor with strong industry relationships, insightful strategies, and accurate performance reporting. Distributors' marketing staffs can execute publicity, marketing research, media, promotion, and marketing materials to maximize the value of the content.

Content owners sometimes prefer a smaller, leaner distributor with the expectation of getting more attention. When the owner believes their product is the highest priority to the distributor, it makes for a more productive partnership. The ability to work together can be more important than the size of the minimum guarantee.

PART TWO

Lessons Learned

25 of my best and worst negotiations versus Big Retail, Professional Sports, Streaming Platforms, TV Cable Networks, Hollywood Studios, and Celebrities.

CHAPTER 10

Negotiation Stakeholders in Crisis

How to Survive, Adapt, and Thrive in Disruption

Disruption #1: Tylenol Poisonings and Product Recall

My first job was field sales with Johnson & Johnson/McNeil, makers of *Tylenol*, the number-one selling over-the-counter pain relief medication. On September 29, 1982, eight people in Chicago died from ingesting *Tylenol* capsules laced with cyanide. McNeil pursued a *compromise negotiation strategy* with law enforcement, hospitals, and retailers. All *Tylenol* manufacturing facilities were made available for the FBI to investigate. McNeil self-initiated a total product recall destroying 31 million *Tylenol* packages while refunding stores and hospitals hundreds of millions of dollars. Wall Street, the media, and business experts gave little hope the brand or company could survive.

The investigation eventually uncovered someone put potassium cyanide poison into the capsules of seven packages of *Tylenol* Extra Strength Capsules 100s. The public perception of McNeil changed from *responsible* to *victim of a terrorist act*. The product recall, credit refunds, and FBI cooperation demonstrated McNeil's *integrity* and regained the *trust* of our partners and consumers.

The media coverage on *Tylenol* included methods for copycat poisonings, which created safety concerns for all retailers and consumer product companies. This shared vulnerability created an edge for McNeil to evolve to a *collaborative negotiation strategy*. Having a head start in tamper-resistant packaging development, retailers and hospitals now wanted McNeil to lead the industry and quickly introduce a safer packaging solution. McNeil met with the medical industry leadership to gain insights how to regain the trust of key influencers: doctors and patients. During a crisis, there needs to be a solid foundation of trust among all parties to have productive *collaborative multiparty negotiations*.

Once McNeil had a viable tamper-resistant packaging solution, the collaborative strategy shifted to a *competitive strategy* with three negotiation goals: Getting media to support the relaunch, regaining retail and hospital distribution, and convincing consumers to trust the brand. The media gave positive coverage of the *Tylenol* publicity campaign announcing the relaunch of the new tamper-resistant packaging featuring the tagline, "Trust *Tylenol*. Hospitals Do." The campaign's spokesperson was the *Tylenol* medical director, who generated instant credibility because not only was he a medical doctor, but he closely resembled the actor Robert Young of the long-running *Marcus Welby MD* TV show. There are many ways to produce trust!

Survive, Adapt, and Thrive

As an employee, deciding whether to leave a company in a crisis is difficult because you don't have visibility to the full details of the negotiated rescue plan. Your immediate responsibility is to help management reduce the downside by providing input and executing the plan. Colleagues venting their emotions disrupt your rational thought and decision making. Your decision to stay or leave is dependent on whether management has established *trust* and *integrity*. This will be evident in how they negotiate with outside entities and communicate with you. Gaining this unique crisis management experience made staying with the company the right thing for my career. McNeil management's negotiating skills saved the company and made the retail industry safer for shopping.

Having survived, I needed to adapt by developing new skills while exceeding expectations performing the recovery plan. My new skill was pursuing my MBA degree with the goal of moving into marketing. I overperformed my objectives as *Tylenol* was able to regain the leading market share in *just four months after the crisis*. These new skills and unique disruption experience made me a better executive and created value for me in the market.

Lessons Learned From the Tylenol Disruption

- Know the best time to begin negotiating.
- Negotiation strategies evolve over time.
- In a crisis, be the first to establish integrity and trust among all stakeholders.
- Get your stakeholders support by soliciting their input and keeping them updated.
- Stakeholders in crisis: respect the company's hierarchy, take direction, and execute.
- Survive by outperforming your colleagues with integrity and fair play.
- Adapting requires executing the new direction while learning new skills.
- Thriving depends on expanding your responsibilities and executing above expectations.

Disruption #2: *The Barbarians at the Gate,* KKR Acquisition of RJR NABISCO

In 1988, RJR Nabisco CEO Ross Johnson needed to do something drastic. The anticipation of a damning cigarette product liability legal decision was depressing the stock value despite strong RJR cash flow and growing Nabisco market share. Still, Johnson sensed the friendly board of directors was getting frustrated by the stagnant stock price.

Johnson decided his best choice for his survival was to negotiate a management buyout of RJR Nabisco using a *competitive strategy* in a zero-sum negotiation. Johnson believed he had the negotiation edge, so he gave a low-ball offer to buy the company. The board hesitated to accept the offer as they were conflicted between their fiduciary duties and loyalty to Johnson. The delay gave time for other entities to submit competitive bids for the company. The fiduciary responsibilities of the board won over their loyalties and led them to put the company up for auction.

Johnson's obvious mistake was being overly confident the deal would be quickly accepted. His biggest error was not including key stakeholder Nabisco president John Greeniaus to his management buyout team.

Johnson considered him *just an employee*. Greeniaus knew Nabisco had more upside potential than Johnson was offering. He survived, adapted, and thrived by going to one of the competitive bidders, Kohlberg, Kravitz, and Roberts (KKR) with justification for a higher price for Nabisco. With this information, KKR now had the negotiation edge to outbid Johnson's offer. KKR, with access to highly leveraged funding, eventually won the U.S.$25 billion deal in a poorly executed public auction. The bad behavior of the board of directors, Ross Johnson, and KKR was later exposed in the best-selling book and Emmy-winning movie, *Barbarians at the Gate*.

Survive, Adapt, and Thrive

The KKR acquisition put Lou Gerstner as CEO to run the company, and our work environment changed overnight. The RJR Nabisco business objectives completely changed. The revenue and market share growth objectives changed to cash flow and profit maximization. At the time, I was managing the Nabisco cracker business (*Ritz* and *Premium*) and launching new products (*Teddy Grahams* and *Ritz Bits Sandwiches*).

KKR wanted to change the culture and *right-size* the company after the deal closed. They executed an amazing plan to accomplish both company goals simultaneously. The plan was to move into a new office building and reduce the workforce by 30 percent the same day. The process began on a Thursday afternoon with packing up our offices in company supplied containers. The red box was for company property, and the white box was for our personal items. The moving company would pickup and deliver both sets of boxes to the new office building later that night.

The next morning at 8 o'clock sharp, Gerstner briefly addressed the Nabisco employees at the Hilton Hotel ballroom located across the parking lot of our new office building. His clear and direct speech set the tone for the new company. Nabisco would have only two objectives for the coming year: cash flow and quarterly profit. The new culture would be one of hard work and the only fun would be getting large cash bonuses by making our financial objectives. There was polite applause as everyone had only one thought on their mind: am I getting laid off this morning?

Gerstner gave the podium to the VP of human resources, who explained the next steps. We were to walk to the lobby of the new building. On the lobby wall were the office seating charts for three floors of employees. If your name was in an office space, you were to go to your office and unpack. If your name was not on the office seating chart, you were to return to the Hilton to pick up your boxed personal belongings and receive your severance package. Those terminated would not be permitted to go inside the new offices. Lastly, there was the reminder a full workday was expected from us. They were serious about not having fun.

A stampede of stylish suits and shoes raced to the new building lobby. People jammed ten-deep around each wall chart as the chatter escalated. No one was moving as we looked for our name and colleagues'. It felt like high school again, finding out if we made the team, the band, or a role in the school play. I looked for the marketing department offices on the chart. There it was, "Mike Saksa – Ritz / New Product Marketing." I had survived.

The lobby sounds changed to muffled swear words and sobbing. The tone evolved into a funeral setting with condolences and hugs. Those who made the cut, became uncomfortable and ascended the stairs to their new offices. Those left behind, tried to compose themselves before taking the walk of shame back to the Hilton Hotel to receive their exit packages and new lives.

To adapt and thrive, I needed to develop new skills and exceed expectations performing the recovery plan. My plan was to work for one year, maximize my bonus, and enter the MFA program at the USC Cinema/TV graduate school. My goal was to transition my skills to the movie business.

We adapted by raising cracker prices three times and drastically cutting costs. We reduced the thickness of the cardboard packaging and plastic sleeves encasing the crackers along with using less salt and spray oil on the crackers. All advertising and consumer promotions were cut. Business travel was reduced to essential meetings only. The first year we made our financial objectives, I received the maximum bonus and everyone was a winner. Surprisingly, the biggest winner was ex-CEO Ross Johnson, who lost the negotiation and walked away with $53 million. I eventually went to work for Warner Bros. (WB) Studio thinking disruptions were in my past.

Lessons Learned From RJR Nabisco Disruption

- The support of internal and external stakeholders is critical for success.
- The most important employees in the company are your direct reports.
- Disruption requires a change in culture and compensation to be successful.
- When disruption is evident, research and develop Plan B for better internal opportunities and Plan C for external opportunities.

Disruption #3: AOL Acquisition of TW Disaster

By 2000, Time Warner (TW) growth was driven by movies, music, TV production, and the recently launched DVD. WB, the crown jewel of TW, was the market leader in theatrical and home entertainment. The movie business was experiencing unprecedented revenue growth from movie libraries being released for the first time on DVD. The studios and creative talent were making more money than ever. TW executive salaries and large year-end cash bonuses were growing by double-digit percentages. Yet, TW management was still unsatisfied with the direction of the company and their compensation.

WB Culture and Compensation

The WB year-end cash bonus distribution methodology was established in the Warner Communication era of the 1980s. Each WB division president had the stature of crown princes with their own building on the studio lot and full discretion allocating the bonus pool to their staff. CEO Steve Ross would give each president a lump sum of money for their division. The presidents would take their *fair* share, and the balance would be allocated to their direct reports. The process would be repeated down the line of management where even the lowest staff would get a cash bonus. The discretionary bonus allocation created a dedicated and loyal staff to the division presidents.

This culture created a healthy competition among the divisional fiefdoms for resources and compensation. Cooperation between divisions was negotiated on a *what's in it for me* basis. All cooperative synergy came with a price to pay. This internal competitive culture drove growth and accountability across all divisions.

The technology sector had a different culture and compensation. Tech companies had a collaborative culture and used stock options as a large part of employee compensation. Companies, like AOL, were making their mid-level managers *paper millionaires*, with large annual stock option allocations. By the late 1990s, TW senior management and employees badly wanted to get stock options in addition to cash bonuses. TW CEO Jerry Levin was more focused on the future direction of the company.

Technology's Threat and Opportunity

TW's Levin was concerned about the sustainability of old media. There was an emerging digital revolution building with the capability to deliver content directly to homes. Levin was eager to have TW establish a comprehensive digital platform to promote its content and eventually sell directly to consumers. WB had failed with multiple internal attempts to build an online presence in the 1990s.

By 1999, Levin felt the urgency to make a deal with an outside digital entity. He quietly developed a relationship with AOL CEO Steve Case, who had a similar vision how technology would grow the entertainment industry. TW had been looking for a way to participate more completely in the digital revolution, while AOL wanted to convert its high stock price into content and other tangible assets. Their relationship fostered three ingredients for a successful negotiation: *a shared vision, integrity,* and *mutual trust.*

A Badly Negotiated Deal

Case and Levin met a few times before an expanded group worked to negotiate AOL's purchase of TW for stock and cash. The negotiations were *collaborative* to the point where the deal was often labeled as a merger instead of an acquisition. The structure of the deal was important because as the acquirer, AOL did the due diligence on TW and not the other way.

In January 2000, AOL agreed to acquire TW for U.S.$164 billion. The deal made Steve Case Chairman of the Board and Levin the CEO of the new AOL Time Warner (AOLTW). A year later, the FTC and the FCC approved the deal on January 11, 2001. Due to the larger market capitalization, AOL shareholders would get 55 percent and TW shareholders 45 percent despite TW having greater annual revenues (U.S.$5 billion versus U.S.$15 billion) and earnings (U.S.$168 million versus U.S.$762 million).

Disaster Ensues

In just one year, the performance of the AOL division crashed due to the growth of high-speed broadband and declining advertising revenues. An SEC investigation of AOL for improper recognition of revenue followed. In just the first year, AOLTW reported a loss of U.S.$99 billion, *the largest loss ever reported by a U.S. company.* The total AOLTW value went from U.S.$241 billion to about U.S.$28 billion. All employee stock options were now worthless. The divisional presidents, expecting to be mega millionaires from the acquisition, now saw their wealth evaporating.

Failure Explained

The main cause for the failure was the integrity of AOL business conditions. The critical negotiation error was the lack of understanding of the two organizations' different cultures (competitive versus collaborative) and compensation (cash bonus versus stock options). The disregard for the culture and compensation differences led to the erroneous assumption that all AOLTW divisions would work together for the shared common good: to increase the AOLTW stock price.

Culture and Compensation Kills Synergy

Chief operating officer Robert Pittman tried in vain to use the content marketing campaigns of WB, HBO, and Turner Networks to increase AOL awareness. The strategy expected to create more views, thereby generating higher ad revenue and eventually raising the company stock price.

But, the collaborative marketing campaigns had trouble gaining companywide acceptance. No TW divisional marketing executive, of which I was one, wanted to dilute the campaigns and have it negatively impact their performance and cash bonus. WB marketing executives would sit across the table from AOL marketing executives jealous of their much larger stock options. Pittman wanted to give up TW marketing resources to enhance the AOL brand for the *greater good of the stock price*. If the strategy worked, AOL executives would get more stock, and TW executives would underperform and get smaller cash bonuses. The strategy never got traction among the TW executives.

AOLTW COO Bob Pittman lost credibility across the company. The TW divisional president's crown prince management style had decentralized his authority. TW division presidents ignored his direction, and the value of AOL brand spiraled down. In 2002, CEO Levin was the first to resign. Pittman's resignation soon followed. Chairman Steve Case resigned in 2003 under pressure from the board. In just two postmerger years, three of the top four executives resigned, and TW dropped the AOL name.

Survive, Adapt, and Thrive

By 2002, many top WB executives left as their stock options were underwater, and TW business fundamentals were broken. I was in a good situation at WB as I was part of the team that had launched DVD. I decided to stay through the disruption because of what I learned from my previous experiences with *Tylenol* and *Nabisco*. Disruption, if handled correctly, creates more opportunities and upward mobility for middle management.

The key is to develop skills that directly benefit growth areas of your organization. Target a position in the highest *growth* or *profit* business units. Avoid being in middle management grinding on a no-growth, mediocre-sized business with little visibility to top management. WB Home Entertainment (WBHE) division was both a high-margin business and revenue growth driver of the new TW company. The highly profitable DVD business was expected to grow and lead the transition to digital delivery of movies and TV shows.

To thrive, I needed to develop a valued skill for the new environment. I knew the studio was not producing enough content to achieve the aggressive growth targets. WBHE would need to acquire content from outside the studio system. Someone with advanced negotiation skills would be needed to lead the effort. I convinced my divisional president to send me to the University of Pennsylvania and Harvard Graduate Business Schools for *Leadership* and *Advanced Negotiations* executive training. When I returned, I was given the responsibilities to lead content acquisitions. By surviving and adapting a new skill, I was able to rise from the rubble of the AOLTW ashes.

Lessons Learned From the AOLTW Disruption

- The side that wants the deal more will pay more and/or assume the most risk.
- Take the necessary time to thoroughly vet the assumptions from both sides.
- Culture and compensation are critical to overcome adversity and ensure success.
- Expecting synergy in the negotiation rarely comes to fruition.
- Develop unique skills to gain a significant role in the highest profit or growth areas.

CHAPTER 11

Negotiating Versus Big Retail

Wal-Mart, Target, and Amazon

Retailer Vendor Agreements

Beginning new business relationships with Big Retail requires negotiating the *vendor agreement*, a contract of operational and financial commitments. Big Retail will insist on a signed vendor agreement prior to buying and receiving inventory. The firm order deadline establishes their initial negotiation edge in this zero-sum *competitive negotiation*. The vendor accepts most of the financial and legal risks such as shipping costs, returns, and payment terms. Big Retail will resist any changes because they cannot manage multiple customized vendor agreements. They have the negotiation edge throughout the relationship because the vendor demand for their retail space and store traffic is greater than the consumer demand for your product.

Big Retail's Negotiation Edge

You can expect the cost of doing business with Big Retail to become more expensive as your success increases. They want you to be successful the first year so that they can increase *their* share of *your* profit as the relationship continues. Big Retail makes small vendors millions in the year one, then slowly leverages down the vendor's profitability in subsequent years. Vendors will justify the diminishing relationship because it *covers a lot of overhead* and *creates brand awareness*. Big Retail will increase their margin in many ways beyond getting lower prices from the vendor.

You need to understand the fundamentals of dealing with Big Retail before entering a vendor agreement.

Big Retail: All Gets With Few Gives

Every business relationship has *gives and gets*, but Big Retail gets most of the *gets* with very few *gives*. Their business relationship is based on getting the *lowest* cost possible and taking the *longest* time to pay in exchange for selling your product in their locations. But there are many other costs along the way where they increase their operating margin:

- Shelf space (slotting allowance)
- Incremental or preferred space (display allowance)
- In-house media department (coop advertising)
- Shipping charges to their distribution centers/stores (shipping cost)
- Returns: handling and shipping charges from stores to distribution centers to your warehouse (returns allowance)
- Marketing to generate the highest number of transactions (development fund)
- On-location consultancy to collect data on your category (category management)

This is a one-sided relationship. The bigger the retailer; the bigger the edge. Every year, new vendors enter into a retailer vendor agreement with unrealistic optimism only have the product perform moderately and lose money. This chapter is what I learned the last three decades doing business with three Big Retailers: Wal-Mart, Amazon, and Target.

Wal-Mart: Tell Us When We Are Not Being Good Partners

Your first experience with Wal-Mart is flying into NW Rogers Airport. There are a limited number of direct flights from major coastal cities into Bentonville. Most flights connect through the Dallas or Kansas City airport. The weather is unpredictable, and many times, there are flight delays or cancelations. It is safest to arrive the day before and stay at the Bentonville Marriot next to the Wal-Mart HQ. Be aware that bad weather can force you to spend a second night. The extra time will give you the full Wal-Mart experience as the Marriot lobby bar is filled with anxious vendor executives and sales personnel talking about their Wal-Mart negotiation experiences.

NW Rogers Airport

NW Rogers Airport, located on the outskirts of Bentonville, Arkansas is "The Unhappiest Place on Earth." The crowded terminal has two types of people. One is the *premeeting sales reps*, who dread the upcoming Wal-Mart meeting knowing they will be getting leveraged for lower prices in a subtle *take it or leave it* competitive negotiation. The other type is the *postmeeting sales reps*, who just had their Wal-Mart meeting, and are trying to find the right time and words to inform the home office of the lower product costs or higher fees.

It gets worse if the postmeeting flight is canceled. You will be wait-listed for the next available flight out. There is a low probability of getting on the next flight because you're competing with hundreds of sales reps with the highest of airline preferred status. Without a superpremium status, you will sit for hours on plastic stools consuming salt, fat, sugar, and caffeine—the staples of a Civil War soldier's diet.

Wal-Mart Headquarters Culture

The Wal-Mart HQ reflects their culture of everyday low price (EDLP). Every vendor, regardless of status, goes to the spartan lobby, signs in, and waits for their buyer to escort them to the meeting room. The meeting rooms have *church basement décor* of linoleum floors, metal chairs, and a folding catering table. A pitcher of water with paper cups is the refreshment. If you bring coffee, snacks, or lunch to the meeting, each Wal-Mart attendee will pay you for their share of the food costs. Wal-Mart has a strict policy of not allowing buyers to be entertained or receive gifts.

My worst Wal-Mart negotiation experience was during the launch of DVD. Six of us traveled to four retailer meetings in three cities over three nights. We flew on a Warner Bros. jet and rented a limousine from the airport to the Wal-Mart HQ to make an early morning meeting. The limo parked near the HQ's front door. The Wal-Mart lobby personnel saw it and word spread quickly. During the meeting, the Wal-Mart buyer demanded lower DVD costs because "our margins being so high we could afford limousines and private jets!" We learned to never arrive to a Wal-Mart meeting in style.

The Wal-Mart Negotiating Edge

Every new Wal-Mart vendor starts with the optimism of being in 4,000 stores, which creates the expectations of selling millions of dollars' worth of goods. The optimism increases when the Wal-Mart buyer opens the meeting by saying: "Over 110 million shoppers enter our stores each week" and "We just want to be good partners." These two statements start every meeting like the national anthem at sporting events. The meetings have the constant drum beat request for lower prices, more promotional money, and the subtle threat of returning your inventory. The senior buyer at the close of the meeting will say, "You tell us when we are not being good partners." You can tell them what they need to do better, but the discussion will always circle back to you providing a lower price. Failure to improve sales quickly (i.e., lower your price) will have your inventory returned. Wal-Mart will always be a good partner but only when your product outsells your competition.

When negotiating with Wal-Mart, it is best to protect your downside and cautiously pursue your upside. Avoid the error of believing your product will sell above their forecast. Sales velocity below the Wal-Mart forecast creates an edge as they will methodically leverage you for more money. It starts with Wal-Mart having the final say when your product gets shipped back to your manufacturing facility. When your product's weekly performance is less than expected, the stores remove the excess inventory from their shelves and place it in the backroom. The product will be shipped to the Wal-Mart distribution center where it issues a credit invoice, plus a charge for shipping and handling.

You can avoid this situation by preemptively lowering your price. Giving Wal-Mart *price protection* on the existing store inventory to get a lower retail price with the expectation of immediately improving consumer sales. You pay Wal-Mart the difference of the current cost and the new lower cost on all inventory. The price protection payment has no guarantee it will work, but failure to lower the price in a timely manner will initiate the product returns. Your financial analysis will usually lead you to lowering the price to create hope for sales improvement versus no action and taking the return.

You are now in the *Wal-Mart quicksand* of repeatedly lowering price to prevent a return. You provide them with the lowest price you never knew you had. Eventually you will have to say no and take the returned inventory. In May 2005, Wal-Mart surprised DreamWorks by returning a large amount of Shrek 2 DVD inventory, which hurt the DreamWorks earnings and stock price.

Wal-Mart is willing to help you keep your optimism in check by testing your new product in a six-month, 100-store test. You pay all the costs, including 100 percent product returns. They will not be overly concerned with your order quantities but more focused on getting the lowest cost. If your product sells well, the store count will be slowly expanded, until sales underperform the target. When sales taper off, they will recommend a lower consumer price to improve sales. Failure to lower your cost will signal Wal-Mart to return all your inventory and conclude your product failed.

Wal-Mart Buyer Negotiation Strategy

Another Wal-Mart's *negotiation edge* is having the best information systems. The buyers and store managers know where each piece of inventory is located and its carrying cost on an hourly basis. Don't be fooled by the buyer's appearance or perceived lack of sophistication. The intent is to make you feel confident and comfortable, so you lower your guard. They use a *competitive* strategy hidden inside a *collaborative* façade.

The Wal-Mart buyers have specific roles to leverage their edge. The senior buyer does most of the talking and ensures there is a perception of a *collaborative relationship*. They are big picture people who highlight the reliance on their world-class information systems and stress the importance of everyday low consumer price. The senior buyer's special skill is motivating you to create a *product exclusive,* a customized version of your best-selling product specifically for Wal-Mart. Sometimes it makes business sense to create an exclusive product to improve your margin as there is little chance of ever raising your price to Wal-Mart.

The junior buyer is focused on getting the lowest price possible by reinforcing the advantages of the "4,000 stores and 110 million shoppers per week." At your year-end review, Wal-Mart buyers inform all the vendors they want lower prices in the coming year. Whichever company delivers the lowest price and the highest retail margin per unit gets preferential in-store treatment. It creates the opportunity for the vendor to start their year with great results. Failure to comply will put you at a disadvantage versus your competition. You find it hard to resist walking toward the Wal-Mart quicksand.

Wal-Mart Store Managers

Wal-Mart store managers are the masters of their domain and responsible for their own financial results (i.e., store profit). Financial discipline and information systems at the store level are the key reasons Wal-Mart dominates retail. Hearing you have support from the 4,000 stores is a misperception. Individual stores are not required to participate in HQ-driven initiatives if the store manager has better use of the space. To justify the situation, Wal-Mart buyers use the same soundbite, "We don't force the Alabama stores to sell snow blowers in October."

The store manager's discretion can make a good HQ opportunity turn into financial quicksand in just one week. The buyer gets you to invest *development funds* to buy a standalone display with hopes that it will generate significantly higher sales. In just a few days, if sales are lower than forecast, the stores' information systems will signal the store manager to remove it because a faster-selling or higher-margin product needs the space. Now your display is sitting in the back room waiting to be returned. Sometimes the better financial decision is to have the product and display destroyed so that you don't have to pay for handling returns.

The quicksand gets deeper when you are too slow to make the decision to price protect your retail inventory. The inventory sitting in the backroom goes to the Wal-Mart distribution center and then back to your company's distribution center. Now you decide to price protect the retail inventory, you ship the new product, at the lower price, to the Wal-Mart stores. Essentially, you are paying two shipments of the product to keep your retail presence. So, when the buyer suggests lowering the retail inventory price, the decision must be done quickly. Wal-Mart creates the deadline and leverages the edge.

Exploding Opportunity Trap

Wal-Mart buyers are very good at negotiating the *exploding competitive opportunity*. If your sales drop below expectations despite being on a display or having premium shelf space, the Wal-Mart buyer will go to your competitors with an opportunity to replace your space if they provide a lower cost. The competitor will do a very quick financial analysis to determine the breakeven. The results often lead to accepting the deal because if they don't accept, the competitor will no longer be the first choice for these quick deals. Companies try for years to get first position for these opportunities. When the competitive vendor accepts the deal, your product will be quickly removed from the store and returned to your warehouse. There is no cause for alarm or an over-reaction as you will have the same opportunity the next quarter. This brilliant cycle of exploding negotiated opportunities continually generates lower costs and higher margins for Wal-Mart.

Dispute Resolution

The resolution of business disputes is another area where Wal-Mart buyers excel in *competitive negotiations*. These deductions tend to grow into millions of dollars of unresolved disputes. Wal-Mart will take an invoice deduction when there is a prolonged cost disagreement or miscommunication. The situation occurs mostly with price discounts when there is ambiguity in the guidelines or tracking is inaccurate. Wal-Mart has been known to refuse to recognize a vendor's price increase and deducts the difference to maintain the lower old price. This forces vendors to use their promotional funds to offset the difference.

To resolve the dispute favorably for them, Wal-Mart will wait until the vendor has new leadership, either a new president or senior sales executive. At that time, Wal-Mart will insist on a resolution, which tests the new person's abilities. Wal-Mart will either threaten to remove the product line or continue to deduct and build on the credit amount. The only flexibility offered is which quarter the payment to Wal-Mart will be required. The new vendor president usually ends up paying and then assigning blame on the previous executive's shortcomings.

Superman Returns ... Literally

Wal-Mart enjoys working with vendors to develop new business models and arrangements to increase their profitability with minimal risk to them. They are willing to take on a new venture—as long as they have no financial exposure. As the Warner Bros. Home Entertainment general manager, I experienced one painful new *business model* lesson. In 2006, I agreed to sell Wal-Mart 2.5 million units of *Superman Returns* DVD at 20 percent below-market price in exchange for never having inventory returned or paying for a price markdown. Legally we were able to sell it at below market because it was a test agreement of the *no return for the life of the product.*

We expected Wal-Mart would take their normal product margin by selling it for U.S.$13, well below the market price of U.S.$16. We expected the other retailers would match Wal-Mart's low consumer price. However, our *good partner* decided to make a margin grab. Wal-Mart sold *Superman Returns* DVD for U.S.$15.50, the going market price. Sales were a disappointing 1.5 million units leaving an excess of one million units at retail.

The store managers followed the vendor agreement and not the returns hold test. The Wal-Mart buyers could not stop the store managers from returning product. One million units of excess inventory was returned to the Wal-Mart distribution center where it sat for years, as legally, WB could not take returns on this title. The issue remained unresolved as Wal-Mart accused WB of overshipping inventory of a mediocre DVD title. Warner Bros. accused Wal-Mart of being too greedy by setting the initial consumer pricing too high.

Lesson Learned From Wal-Mart

- Wal-Mart uses a competitive negotiation strategy hidden inside a collaborative facade.
- Understand the Wal-Mart vendor agreement and culture to be successful.
- Cautiously pursue your upside and aggressively protect your downside.
- The longer you deal with Wal-Mart, the more realistic your expectations will become.
- Once you begin shipping to Wal-Mart, they control the product and your fate.

TARGET: They've Got Style, Taste, and Innovation

Target Department Stores are on the other end of the retailer spectrum from Wal-Mart. Their HQ is in the center of a cosmopolitan city, Minneapolis, and everything about them exudes youth, style, and taste. The Target buyers are acutely focused on product knowledge and their primary shopper trends—suburban females. The only similarities between Target and Wal-Mart are the HQ visitor procedures and vendor agreements. The décor of the Target lobby is big photos, bright colors, and bold graphics. The youthful employees are dressed in the latest fashions and newest trends. It's like the *Wizard of Oz*, where Wal-Mart is the black and white Kansas farm scenes and Target is the colorful city of Oz.

The Negotiation Sheriffs

In the late 1990s, record companies and retailers were being investigated for price fixing because of the label's trade promotions on CDs required a minimum advertised price (MAP). This discouraged any retailer from offering an extremely low price for an advertised CD. Movie studios wanted to avoid the investigation expanding to their advertising policy for DVD.

Target recognized the record label and movie studio meetings needed to avoid any suggestion of retail price fixings, so they developed an innovative negotiation process for their entertainment enterprise buying team.

All entertainment meetings would include the buyers and two negotiators, one from finance accounting and the other from business affairs. The buyers ran the meeting, focusing on movie content and order quantities. The Target negotiators would take over when discussing costs, in-store placement, and promotional funding. These skilled negotiators were effective at leveraging the Target assets to get the most out of the studios' promotional spending. They documented the spending with a specific merchandising plans, forecasts, and scorecards. The movie studios knew exactly what was required and the cost. There were no discussions on consumer retail pricing, which avoid any appearance of price fixing.

Auction Replaces Buying

Target developed a second negotiation innovation for their entertainment enterprise buying team. The traditional buying process for DVD display space was a two-month *collaborative negotiation*. Target buyers would inform each of the six studios of the available space and have multiple discussions on titles, costs, and placement fees. The displays would have a mixture of movie titles from various studios at different costs. The financial risk fell on the buyer's ability to get the optimal title selection and pricing.

Target management changed the buying process to a *competitive negotiation* by implementing an online blind auction for monthly DVD display space. On a designated day and time, an auction website was made available to the studios. The site provided the details of a future display location, size, and consumer retail price. The blind bidding was open for one hour. The firm deadline required the studios to quickly determine the financial feasibility for their bid. The site had a running list of the anonymous leading bid and time remaining in the auction. At the end of the hour, the anonymous bid with the lowest cost to Target won the display space.

Target knew the studios' competitiveness would generate aggressive bids. In the closing minute, bidders' emotions created such a frenzy, the winning bid would often be unprofitable for the studio. They could not resist outbidding each other. Target had created a negotiation process where the winner would lose. This brilliant innovation by Target minimized their product cost and put the financial risk on the studios. It took years for the studios to develop the negotiation skills to make these auctions profitable.

Lessons Learned From Target

- Building a negotiating team with superior special skills creates an edge.
- Auctions generate higher revenue in a zero-sum negotiation with a short time period.
- Every negotiation has an optimal strategy, but it can evolve over time.

Amazon—The Smartest People in the Room

The record labels and movie studios business practice with retailers is to release new content on Tuesdays. The retail staff gets three days to build displays and stock the new release sections before the weekend—the busiest retail days. The new content increases store traffic on the slowest retail day of the week. The Tuesday release date is a contractual firm date that keeps all retailers on a level playing field. If a retailer sold a CD, DVD, or digital download before the Tuesday, there would be financial penalties.

Third-Party Seller Competition

Amazon was competitive with other retailers by creating a preorder system delivering the new release DVD to homes on street date. This required movie studios to ship new release inventory to Amazon warehouses weeks in advance of the release date, despite the increased risk of counterfeiting. Amazon quickly began to gain market share from competition. A few years later, Amazon began their third-party consignment model where they would warehouse products from other companies, take orders, and ship them to consumers for a 30 percent distribution fee. This was a better proposition than the 10 percent margin buying new release DVDs directly from the studios.

On the Amazon preorder site, the studios noticed their new releases priced below cost from small, unknown companies. The studios could not determine how these small companies received their DVD product. A studio investigation revealed the deep-discounted DVDs were counterfeit copies and almost indistinguishable from the authentic studio product. The copies were selling well and cannibalizing the studios' direct shipments to Amazon, costing the studios millions of dollars of revenue.

Each studio met separately with Amazon to resolve the problem. Studio attendees were high-level executives and attorneys, while Amazon sent two mid-level buyers to the meetings. The side with the higher-level people has the greater need for progress. Not having your decision maker at a contentious meeting is an effective negotiation avoidance and delay tactic that allowed Amazon to continue to reap the benefits of the high margin third-party sales.

The studios wanted Amazon to examine the inventory, identify the counterfeit products, and shut down the third parties from selling allegedly stolen intellectual property. The studio attorneys believed Amazon was committing a felony by selling stolen goods. Amazon's resistance had a three-fold explanation:

- The third-party sellers own the inventory and require permission to inspect their products.
- Amazon does not have the resources to inspect the third-party inventories.
- The Amazon DC personnel are untrained and could not determine an authentic studio DVD product from the counterfeit copy.
- The Amazon's solution was for the studios to adjust their pricing to match the 30 percent margin and they would discontinue DVD third-party sales.

The HBO executive was particularly incensed at the Amazon position because the biggest counterfeit sales were impacting the highly profitable *Game of Thrones* DVD. This angered the HBO executive, who responded they had no other choice but to notify the California Attorney General of the situation. The buyer was nonplussed and responded, "Jeff (Bezos) already met with them, and I think we're good."

Meeting Room Negotiation Edge

Amazon knows how to create the edge using meeting room attendance. Meetings with Amazon were always crowded as everyone wanted to have the *Amazon experience* on their resume. Amazon would have only one or two executives in attendance. They knew in large meetings the ego-centric studio executives would compete with each other trying to prove who was smarter and more valuable to the account. This behavior resulted in Amazon receiving excessive amounts of information and commitments. The more undisciplined people attending on one side of the table, the more information travels one way. Advantage Amazon.

The Report Card

Another disadvantage of one-side crowding the negotiation room is the vulnerability to criticism. Amazon gave each studio a year-end report card on their performance versus competition. The annual meetings were held in January at the Consumer Electronics Show in Las Vegas. Amazon would invite the head of the studio and their executive team to recap their calendar year with a report card and set plans for the coming year.

With the growth of DVD, each studio expected a great report card. Studios looked forward to the meeting as a good report card would support a bigger year-end bonus for studio executives. Amazon started the meetings by prompting the studio president to talk first. This person would talk about accomplishments, what a great partner Amazon is, and how they looked forward to working with Amazon in the coming year. The crowded studio side of the table was all smiles and full of positive reinforcement.

Then Amazon would thank the studio for the hard work and commitment, but expressed the studio was not supporting Amazon to the level of their competition. The report card would be put up on the monitor showing how poorly the studio was in many key categories versus the other studios. The Amazon executive would go down each failed performance metric and elicit specific commitments on how much better the studio could do in the coming year. The room would go silent as the embarrassed studio head looked to the staff with the "how did this go so wrong" look. This tactic put the studio on the defense with the only way to save face was to overcommit on the spot to meet Amazon's needs. When satisfied, Amazon would quickly end the meeting, leaving the shocked studio executives to blame each other for the bad report.

Lessons Learned From Amazon

- They appear to be collaborative negotiators but compete with their superior analytics.
- The smartest people in the room are the ones with the superior preparation and data.
- The smaller the negotiating team, the better chance to control the discussion.
- More people in the meeting creates vulnerability and less opportunity for progress.
- Providing a scorecard of the other side's performance puts you on the offensive.
- Not having your decision-making executives attend a contentious meeting is an effective negotiation delay tactic.

CHAPTER 12

Negotiating Professional Sports Content

Part One: The NFL and NBA

Competing for Content

By early 2001, movie studio DVD revenues were growing exponentially. The Warner Bros. large slate of new movies and TV shows plus the massive library were not enough content to achieve the corporate growth targets. The home entertainment division needed to go outside the studio to acquire independent content in a highly competitive market. All the studios were aggressively looking for additional content and willing to overpay for it. The smaller studios: Sony, Paramount, and Lionsgate were trying to convince independent producers they would better nurture their content and deliver better results. Convincing content owners that *bigger is better* was going to be our challenge.

Distribution Strategy

As the negotiation leader, I utilized a *collaborative negotiation strategy* by reinforcing our abilities to work together to create something bigger and better. We wanted to demonstrate early in the process how WBHE would provide better service. A key tactic was attending every meeting and presenting the plan to utilize our large marketing, sales, financial accounting, and strategic planning departments to deliver four distribution strategies:

- Generate market and consumer research to *identify the best content opportunities.*
- Create impactful *marketing elements* and effective *marketing campaigns.*

- Utilize our industry relationships to maximize *retail space*.
- Provide accurate and timely *reporting of revenue and expenses*.

Professional Sports Leagues

By 2001, the growing interest in sports content was ready to be exploited in the underserved DVD market. The leagues had overlooked the home entertainment opportunity by not having a content strategy or centralized distribution agreements. Sports video content was mainly VHS season highlights produced by the individual teams and distributed in their local markets. The revenue was negligible as teams used these releases mainly to market to their local fan base.

The leagues were now eager to produce and distribute DVD content. The league's licensing departments took control of the game footage from the individual teams and assumed responsibility for negotiating *exclusive* licensing rights.

WBHE Sports Content Strategy

The strategy was to use our scale and industry relationships to release sports content throughout the year in dedicated DVD sports sections in each of the big retailers: Wal-Mart, Best Buy, Target, and Amazon. The plan was to begin negotiations with the NFL and use that agreement to attract the NBA, NHL, and MLB. If successful, we would pursue secondary sports segments such as NASCAR, pro wrestling, PGA golf, college football, and various extreme sports. We wanted to quickly acquire exclusive rights with multiple leagues before the other studios entered the market and drove up the costs. Universal (NBC) and Paramount (CBS) were our main competition for sports content, but they did not have a comprehensive DVD sports strategy or the dedicated resources. The negotiation strategy was to *collaborate* on revenue generation strategies and avoid having to *compete* on the acquisition price.

NFL Negotiations

The NFL's mission is to enhance the brand and grow the revenues of the 32 teams. We approached the NFL to determine their interest in creating new content and distributing to a broad retail base. The negotiations were set up through the NFL licensing division, as the deal would be categorized as *licensing of game footage*. Our plan was to offer a small cash advance and a revenue share deal in exchange for home entertainment exclusivity of game and player profile footage.

The NFL was our first priority due to their popularity and NFL Films. This world-class production unit produced highlight clips for news outlets. They had a large catalog of footage, but no retail market to monetize it other than one-off licensing deals. Historically, NFL Films produced two videos annually: $10 *Follies* and a *Super Bowl Champions*. The latter was offered free with a paid *Sports Illustrated* subscription.

Stakeholder Premeeting

We began the negotiations with a premeeting at the NFL Films offices outside of Philadelphia for strategic reasons. First, we wanted to see the quality and breadth of the available footage. We were amazed by the size of their library of games and behind-the-scenes footage. It was equal in scale and quality to the Warner Bros. movie library. These professionals took their mission of preserving the history of the game seriously. Second, we needed to evaluate the capabilities of the production staff to create content on a quick turnaround. We would need them to create a Super Bowl DVD within 24 hours for us to replicate and ship to 10,000 retail locations one week after the game. The NFL producers showed us their impressive filming and editing process. We concluded NFL Films had the expertise and resources needed to support our sports strategy.

The third reason to meet with NFL Films was to get a sense of our ability to work together. They gave us first-hand insights on what the league wanted in a home entertainment partner. NFL Films wanted to increase their quantity and quality of content and move away from low-priced highlight films offered in sporting goods stores or given away in a mail-order promotion. They wanted to have broad distribution across North America and Europe. They preferred working with a big Hollywood studio because of our creative abilities, ample resources, and an expansive distribution system. Getting direct exposure to the other side's stakeholders provides critical information and gave us an early negotiation edge.

Perhaps, the biggest reason for meeting with NFL Films was to convince them we were the best movie studio for their content. The NFL views themselves as the superior sports league and only work with the best in their respective industries. Their attitude of being the best by working with the best is ingrained in their culture. They only want to partner with the best content creators, marketers, and distributors. They had no concerns about the level of priority from any partner. In this case, we were the ones who were concerned with being a priority within the NFL universe.

At the end of the meeting, we went into auditioning mode by selling our capabilities. Self-promotion is an area in which studios are highly skilled! We wanted to *outprofessional* our competition by demonstrating our industry knowledge, marketing resources, and retail strength. We even went so far as to demonstrate how each of us were NFL enthusiasts and knew their brand attributes. We discussed our vision for a preliminary three-year release schedule of team histories, player biographies, Super Bowl winners, season greatest plays, and eventually, a fantasy league primer. In the end, we knew our efforts had gained the support of an important stakeholder group for the subsequent NFL licensing negotiations.

NFL Negotiation Playbook

The following week we met at the NFL HQ in New York to begin the negotiations. The NFL operated like a Fortune 500 company demonstrating highly professional negotiation room conduct. All their executives wore suits, meetings were run on time with predetermined agendas and follow-up notes. The dynamics were like an actual football game with their premeetings (huddle), negotiation roles (play assignments), and execution of the plan (the play). There were no cheap shots, personal fouls, or unsportsmanlike conduct. Everyone performed their role, input was provided from all sides, approvals proceeded methodically through many layers of management, and ultimately, a three-year deal was sent to the commissioner, Paul Tagliabue, who approved it in a timely manner.

Royalty Fee Structure

The NFL wanted a royalty deal similar to their other NFL licensed vendors. They provide the assets in exchange for a minimum guarantee and a share of the collected net revenue. WBHE would pay the NFL after the recoupment of the advanced minimum guaranteed payment. We would reimburse NFL Films for their production cost and have product ownership, pricing, marketing, and distribution control. The NFL would have *meaningful consultation* throughout the process and creative approval on the final product. The royalty rate was favorable as the NFL perspective was a *licensed consumer product* percentage in the 8 to 10 percent range versus an *entertainment content* percentage range of 12 to 20 percent.

At the signing of the contract, WBHE paid the minimum guarantee based on 50 percent of the projected revenue for a three-year deal. Both sides viewed this as a *prove it* deal as it was an emerging market and considered a *small risk, small reward* agreement. The NFL prioritizes their licensing deals by the size of the minimum guarantee or gross revenue. The WBHE deal was considered a relatively low priority versus TV networks, insurance companies, credit cards, snacks, or beverage deals. The real value of the deal to the NFL was the retail exposure outside of their traditional media channels.

Emerging Market: Protect the Upside and Downside

The NFL and WBHE were entering a partnership in an emerging category. The results could vary widely after three years. Both sides wanted to protect their downside but still participate in the upside. The NFL protected their downside by getting a reasonable minimum guarantee. WBHE protected the downside with the rights to set the retail price and sell off excess inventory at the end of the deal. These sell-off rights would make it difficult for the NFL to get a new partner. The control of inventory and pricing provide a negotiation edge with contract extensions.

There is a need to protect the upside in an emerging category, should the product become a huge success. If the product sold well during the three-year deal, the NFL could go to competitors to get a better deal. As the initial acquirer, you could spend a lot of resources building a business, then have the business walk away for better financial terms. We secured protection by getting the *right of first and last refusal* on any subsequent deals. This means that at the end of the first deal, NFL is required to show WBHE any new competitive deal terms, and we would have the right to match. These clauses are beneficial to both sides as it assures a market rate deal while maintaining the productive working relationship with the partner.

Find the Hidden Costs

Doing business with the NFL had other unique contractual costs in the deal. NFL requires partners to buy a specific number of high-priced Super Bowl tickets, expensive NFL-controlled hotel rooms, and exclusive NFL party passes for the Super Bowl week activities. The individual attendee cost at the Super Bowl summit was $10,000 to $15,000 per person for flights, rooming, games tickets, parties, food, and beverage.

We justified the costs by using Super Bowl week to hold retailer meetings with Best Buy, Target, Amazon, and various video distributors. Retail executives rarely turndown all-expenses-paid trips to Super Bowls, with the exception of Wal-Mart, who prohibit any entertainment or gifts from vendors. Even without the biggest retailer, the meetings were successful on two measures. First, we gained full-year distribution for the NFL titles at all retailers. Second, the retailers became our supportive stakeholders for our upcoming negotiations with the NBA and NHL.

Our first NFL DVD release was the Super Bowl XXXVII with the Raiders versus the Buccaneers in January 2003. Expectations were high as the Raiders have one of the largest fan-bases in the NFL. The entire three-year deal would payout if the heavily favored Raiders won. On the other side, the Buccaneers, had one of the lowest engaged fan bases due to their community demographic and decades of losing. The Buccaneers won in an upset, and we took a financial loss on the first release. My management teased how I had "lost millions on the Super Bowl." Fortunately, we had a multiyear NFL plan. We accelerated our big-market team histories of the *New York Football Giants, Chicago Bears, Dallas Cowboys, New England Patriots,* and *Philadelphia Eagles,* which made the deal financially and creatively rewarding for both parties.

Lessons Learned From the NFL Negotiations

- Collaborative strategy needs mutual respect at the beginning of the negotiation.
- The organization's head person establishes the culture and sets the tone.
- Adapt your negotiation tactics to the level of priority you are for the other side.
- Negotiate shorter-term deals with mutually agreeable extensions in an emerging or volatile marketplace.

NBA Negotiations

The NBA is next biggest sports league with smaller revenue, but higher potential due to their global fan base. The NBA licensing group would lead the negotiations, but the tone would come from Commissioner Daniel Stern, a former attorney with a reputation of a scrappy, tough negotiator. The negotiation would take the form of a basketball game: a physical freelance style with lots of pushing and elbowing.

The Making of a Difficult Negotiation

Right from the start, the scheduling of meetings was challenging. It was not unusual to have a scheduled meeting at WBHE only to have it canceled the day before. If there was a meeting, it was to address their issues of the day. The NBA negotiators rarely documented the discussions and our follow-up notes were either disputed or ignored. This behavior was likely a stall tactic to allow for time to negotiate with other studios. I made an initial error by not having an NDA and an exclusive negotiating time period.

An industry source suggested Stern did not want the same video partner as the NFL, as they were competing for the same young male audience and dollars. We saw the situation differently believing both leagues would release content in different seasons with little overlap. Our schedule would release the NFL content in September–February and the NBA content in December-June. Our retailers wanted to have both leagues managed by the same distributor to ensure optimal release schedules and consistent management in a new category.

The Key Issues

We had three key issues that made us think this deal would not happen. The first issue was their insistence on getting a higher royalty rate than the NFL. That was a nonstarter. Sometimes one side will test your integrity by asking for details of a competitive deal. We honored our NFL nondisclosure agreement and did not to reveal any contract details. We needed to maintain our reputation and ensure the trust of our current and future partners. We countered with an escalating deal structure that would enable the NBA to surpass the NFL agreement if the content quality and sales performance exceeded predetermined levels.

The second issue was wanting the minimum guarantee to be greater than the NFL's. They believed the global appeal of the NBA was greater due to having players from Europe, South America, and Asia. We declined but used the *worldwide business* statement to our advantage as WBHE is the only movie studio with offices throughout Europe, South America, and Asia.

The third issue was the abundance of current NBA DVD inventory in the market. The NBA had numerous nonexclusive deals saturating the market with low-quality, low-priced DVDs. There was no branding or quality consistency. The local teams released whatever they wanted without league oversight. There was an overabundance of Michael Jordan and dunking highlights DVDs. Another competitive challenge to the market was an abundance of low-priced, low-quality content from crowdsourced *Street Highlights*. This was user-generated camcorder footage of playground league play. They also did a team championship DVD giveaway with a *Sports Illustrated* subscription.

We had two very different philosophies on how basketball footage should be managed in the DVD market. The NBA saw the nonexclusive video releases as part of their grass roots marketing. The incremental DVD revenue was found money to the NBA teams. They did not see a need for an exclusive content deal, and if they were to agree, they would not put resources to shut down the pirated footage. We did not want to pay a minimum guarantee only to have our product knocked off by a local distributor.

Resolving the Impasse

A tactic to resolve deal breaker issues is to have an influential stakeholder convince the other side to be your partner. Usually, this stakeholder has a financial stake or operational responsibility in the deal. We encouraged the head buyers of the major retailers to reach out to the NBA negotiators to explain the benefit of WBHE managing the sports section. They explained the need for better retail presentation and inventory management. The NBA eventually agreed to make an *exclusive* deal but would not protect WBHE from teams distributing their own DVDs. The NBA suggested we go to the teams directly and make one-off releases for them as an addendum to the league's deal. This way, we would be able to control the inventory.

With all these outstanding issues, our overall concern with the NBA was our ability to work productively together. Their behavior made us less confident they would follow the deal terms. When there is adversarial behavior in a negotiated agreement, expect similar behavior when a challenging business situation arises. At this point, we did not believe we could productively work with this group.

Revised Engagement Plan

Realizing an equitable deal was not going to happen, we shifted our plan to accelerate the pursuit of other sports deals. Our initial discussions with other sports entities gave us the confidence we could achieve year-round sports content without the NBA. Having the support of the major retailers would ensure we could dominate the retail space. We thought the NBA eventually would see the benefit of partnering with us. If they came back, it would be on our terms.

We broke off talks in a very friendly manner so that it would be easy for us to get back together in the future. The NBA was not surprised when we told them we were going to pursue other content. We wished them the best of luck whichever distributor they chose.

The key strategy when breaking off talks is to keep the other side attracted to you. We knew one of the NBA junior executives wanted the deal because it provided job security, and having a studio deal would help his resume. We wanted him as an *insider stakeholder*. We instructed one of our staff to maintain a business relationship with this person. He was to give the NBA junior executive our market share data, industry sales reports, and pictures of how successful we were building a retail DVD sports section. We gave the exec tickets to WB movie premieres in NYC where he received swag from our theatrical marketing department. We wanted a valuable stakeholder if we were to ever reengage the NBA.

Lessons Learned From the NBA Negotiations

- Understand the other side leader's profile and decision-making process.
- When there is a lack of trust in the negotiations, take control by writing the agendas, documenting all discussions, and distributing the follow-up notes.
- Expect the behavior in the negotiation will be the same behavior working together later.
- Identify who on the other side wants the deal, and use that contact at the optimal time.
- Sometimes, it is better to walk away, but do it in a friendly manner so that returning is not awkward.

CHAPTER 13

Negotiating Professional Sports Content

Part Two: NHL, WCW, NBA (Part 2), and Others

National Hockey League

With the NBA negotiations on hold, we accelerated our discussions with the NHL. Their November to May season was a perfect substitute for the NBA. They were waiting for us and interested in getting a deal done quickly. We viewed the NHL deal as a low-risk, moderate-reward agreement because their existing DVD content was vastly underexploited in the United States market. The only DVD releases were Toronto and Montreal team highlights in Canada. One area of concern was the low NHL TV ratings. The small fan base suggested a low-revenue ceiling.

The NHL negotiation was a friendly collaboration with transparency and trust on both sides. Our research on NHL commissioner Gary Bettman revealed a rational, analytical executive who prefers to work behind the scenes. We aligned our presentation with his decision-making process by providing more data than our competition. The NHL negotiators were very likeable, the kind of guys you want to share a beer. Their casual demeanor was best suited to a collaborative negotiation strategy. Both parties came into the negotiations with realistic expectations. This was not a deal to overnegotiate.

The tone of the negotiations played out like a hockey game: fast-paced, crisp plays, and an emphasis on teamwork. The NHL wanted to have DVD content generating a new revenue stream for the league and increased awareness. WBHE wanted a second major sports league to build out the DVD retail section. We believed there was minimal financial downside as the first release, a documentary on Wayne Gretzky, could pay for the entire deal.

They quickly agreed to an industry standard royalty deal because, "What the hell do we know about DVD?" WBHE would control all aspects of the business and pay the NHL a percentage of the net collected revenues. There was a very small advance paid to the NHL more out of respect than a financial need. In just two meetings over the course of five days, we had a handshake deal in place before Bettman officially signed the deal.

The first release, *Ultimate Wayne Gretzky DVD* was supported by The Great One with premieres in Toronto and Los Angeles. The successful DVD release paid for the entire three-year deal! This was needed because the small market expansion team, the Tampa Bay Lightning, won the championship over the Calgary Flames. Having to release an ice hockey DVD in Tampa in July was tough, knowing we would lose money. But that is why you have a contract. Who would have thought that Tampa Bay would be the city of champions for football and hockey in the first year of our sports deals?

Lessons Learned From the NHL Negotiations

- Establishing integrity and trust early sets a productive tone in any new negotiation.
- Having minimal levels of approvals will decrease negotiation complexity.
- Every deal has upside. Ensure to set the terms for an opportunity to achieve it.

Professional Wrestling (WCW)

One of the benefits of the AOLTW marketing summits was learning about other division's successes such as the Turner Network Television (TNT) and the World Championship Wrestling (WCW). Ted Turner created the WCW by aggregating multiple regional wrestling shows. Professional wrestling is *scripted entertainment* and not a sport. The weekly matches aired on TNT to strong regional ratings. Unlike NASCAR, TNT controlled the video rights to the wrestlers, who would participate in the video revenues. The wrestlers are motivated self-promoters and well-conditioned athletes who perform over 200 events on the road each year. Their work is physically challenging and a mental grind.

A meeting was set up at a live WCW event at the LA Forum with my counterpart at Turner and the WCW producers to begin negotiating a home entertainment deal. *Goldberg* was the current champion, and *Diamond Dallas Paige* was the popular challenger in the main event. The LA Forum was filled with wide a variety of rabid fans from booing middle schoolers to obscenity-yelling grannies. It was helpful to see firsthand the demand for our product prior to a negotiation.

I met Goldberg and Paige in the locker room right before the match as both would benefit from the new deal. Both wrestlers were business-like and did not exhibit the extreme behavior displayed in the ring. As I explained the content strategy, one would walk out of the locker room to the WCW on-site office only to return and calmly sit down. Apparently, that night, the *script* was for Goldberg to lose the championship belt to Page. Goldberg was not in agreement as this would decrease the value of his licensing revenue and personal appearances. He would make more money remaining the champion in the new DVD deal. Prebout renegotiations happen from time to time, and it gets resolved *upstairs*. This night's negotiation was quickly resolved, and we got to witness the entertaining drama of a live scripted athletic event.

The DVD deal terms were quickly negotiated as we had the same corporate management and realistic expectations. TNT would produce all the wrestling content, and WBHE would get the *sister division* terms: a 15 percent distribution fee with no advance required. TNT would own the IP and have approval over all aspects of the business.

WCW *Lesson Learned*

- Having the negotiation observed by your management ensures rationale behavior and productive discussions.
- Avoid overnegotiating when you expect to be in a codependent, long-term relationship.
- The projected value of content deals is derived from fan engagement mathematical models.
- Get to know the talent before the negotiation because the ability to work with them is critical in any content deal.

National Basketball Association
Rebounds: Part Two

Having secured the NFL, NHL, and WCW rights, we needed one more spring or early summer sports DVD to have year-round programing and consistent retail merchandising. We contacted the NBA junior executive to determine if the league would reconsider our last position. We did not realize the NBA was doing the same thing to us but at a much higher level!

I was surprised to receive a call from a Time Warner corporate executive wanting to know why we did not have a deal with the NBA. Turner Network was in negotiations on a multiyear TV deal worth *hundreds of millions* to broadcast NBA games. The NBA was working the back channels to have TW *throw in* a favorable home entertainment deal. The Turner execs were told we were difficult and unwilling to negotiate a fair deal. After I explained the situation, the TW corporate executive explained, "The relationship between TNT and the NBA is much more important than your little DVD business. It is in your best interest to have a home entertainment deal with the NBA as soon as possible." Both TW and Turner Networks believed a deal would create numerous cross-promotion opportunities. I flinched when told to partner with another TW division. It had only been a few years since the AOL acquisition of Time Warner brought the promise of massive synergistic revenue growth. We all know how that worked out.

I reluctantly agreed to re-engage knowing we had lost the negotiation edge. The NBA knew we would have to *compromise*. As the smaller deal, you don't want to be the cause of your bigger partner paying more. We needed to stay out of the way.

We reconnected with the NBA negotiators by providing an updated market conditions and business status. We insisted on the *exclusive licensing* term, which would require the NBA to stop licensing game footage for non-news usage and vigorously defend our rights with counterfeiters. My rationale was that Turner would not accept the airing of any NBA games by another network. The NBA should grant WBHE the same condition. The league needed to establish centralized control as strong as the NFL and NHL deals.

We countered their reluctance by demanding financial safeguards in the three-year deal. First, we wanted a low minimum guarantee to be partially paid before each of the three years. Second, we required a *carryover recoupment clause*, meaning any WBHE shortfall would *carry over* to the following year. At the expiration, the deal would automatically extend until WB recouped its investment for all three years.

We finally agreed to terms, but not before last-minute requests for minor changes from the NBA. We suspected the full deal was in front of David Stern, who wanted a few claw backs. The NBA is like any other business with an omnipotent leader. You don't know where you stand without having direct access. When the negotiation leader and final approver are separate, expect last-minute changes and threats of walking away. The deal was eventually signed with low expectations on both sides.

The NBA was not an immediate success as the first two releases under-performed expectations. The first release was a premium-priced box set, *The History of the Chicago Bulls*, featuring Michael Jordan highlights. Despite the high-quality production, consumer sales were low due to the saturation of Jordan videos in the market. Another explanation was our pricing was too high for the saturated $10 DVDs market. Also, Jordan's popularity was waning, and the NBA had yet to find its next star.

The second release was the *2003 NBA Team Championship San Antonio Spurs*, a small market team with low-profile stars Tim Duncan and David Robinson. They did have two international stars in Argentinian Manu Ginobili and Frenchman Tony Parker, so it made some international revenue. As with any deal, you need to evaluate it for the long term. The next three box sets releases: the *History of the Los Angeles Lakers*, the *History of the Boston Celtics*, and the *History of the Philadelphia 76ers* were successful, and eventually, the three-year deal paid out.

Other Sports Opportunities

Major League Baseball

With the NFL, NBA, NHL, and WCW deals completed, we still wanted a summer season sport to have year-round programing and retail presence. We pursued Major League Baseball (MLB) due to the March–October seasonality and the success of the PBS Ken Burns' *Baseball* DVD box set. We quickly discovered a small independent distribution company had the MLB rights, and some of the teams had their own video rights. We tried to carve-out player highlights or greatest plays of the year rights;

however, the deal became very complex. The other business challenge was the baseball fan base skewed to males 55+ years of age, which was a reluctant DVD consumer demographic. This was a deal with too much legal and commercial risk, so we decided to pass.

NASCAR

Our research on NASCAR had great DVD potential due to their strong TV ratings on the Fox Network and a regional demographic that fit the Wal-Mart consumer. Fox did not own the DVD rights, and there were no NASCAR videos at retail. We quickly developed a content plan for top race highlights and driver biographies.

After numerous conference calls and meetings with NASCAR officials, we finally learned the hard truth. NASCAR did not own their home entertainment video rights. The individual drivers, racing teams, and the racetracks are independent contractors, and each owned their video rights. We made pitches for separate deals with Dale Earnhardt, Jeff Gordon, and Richard Petty along with the popular tracks such as Daytona, Talladega, and Charlotte. We were surprised to learn that any footage would require payments to and approval from *every driver and owner in the race*!

NASCAR car owners and drivers are a very competitive group of individual contractors. No driver wanted to be shown being beaten in any highlight footage. It gave them as much pleasure preventing one of their competitors from making money as it was making money for themselves. How do you show a race without the other cars? Creatively, there is no story to tell without the competitive drama on the track. This was a case of the legal and creative challenges being larger than the business potential. Despite the continued encouragement from our largest retailer, Wal-Mart, we had to abandon our efforts.

PGA Tour

We pursued the video rights of the Professional Golf Association (PGA) tour where Tiger Woods was growing the fan base beyond upper-income, older males. The PGA was another sports organization with complicated video rights issues with the TV networks, the major courses, and the IMG agency, all participating on various levels. We met with IMG representatives who laid out their event video rights and extensive library of golf events. Creatively we could not develop a viable video concept around the patchwork of rights, so we passed on the tour.

CHAPTER 14

Negotiating TV Content

PBS, BBC, and National Geographic

Our market analysis revealed an opportunity gap in our content portfolio: high-quality, niche, branded cable network programing. This content would attract an older, more educated demographic to the DVD market. These distribution deals would also raise the quality perception of WBHE.

Cable TV programs began having great success releasing full seasons on DVD. The phenomenon started with *The Family Guy* in 2003. Although it failed in its first season on the Fox network, it subsequently became a ground-breaking success on DVD. Not only did Fox generate incremental revenue from the sales, but the DVD served as a sampling vehicle for each show. As a result, there was a proliferation of cable networks wanting to broaden their audience reach with DVD releases. Cable TV programs were *low risk–moderate reward* for distributors due to the strong brand and high-quality programing reputation.

Our content strategy, bolstered by the success of DVD, was to extend our current distribution deals with National Geographic (Nat Geo), British Broadcasting Company (BBC), and Public Broadcasting Service (PBS). These deals were financially risky due to their small audiences of only two to three million viewers. A high percentage would need to become DVD consumers to make the deals payout. Another risk is WBHE would have no influence on content production as these networks fill their slates with outside production companies. Occasionally they produce a breakout commercial hit like a PBS *Ken Burns' Baseball* or BBC's *Planet Earth*. We pursued contracts with five-year minimums to increase the probability of getting at least one hit program during the term of the agreement.

PBS

Background

In the late 1990s, PBS came to WBHE with the acquisition of Turner Networks and New Line Cinema. During the due diligence of the acquisition, we became aware of the troubling history of PBS Video division. Our research revealed a company culture of unrelenting management involvement and unrealistic expectations.

In 1990, PBS licensed their exclusive video rights to ex-Monkee Michael Nesmith's Pacific Arts, a relatively new video production and distribution company. Nesmith was an early industry visionary who saw the potential of selling VHS tapes to video rental stores for $65 per cassette. Trouble began when the market shifted to a broader retail distribution. These big retailers required fast and accurate inventory replenishment and returns. The evolving video business model became complex and costly for Pacific Arts.

PBS wanted out of their deal because Pacific Arts was not meeting their expectations in the emerging home entertainment market. In 1994–1995, PBS and five of their content providers: Ken Burns' American Documentaries, WGBH, WNET, Radio Pioneers Film Project, and The Children's Television Workshop filed a lawsuit against Pacific Arts and Nesmith. The plaintiffs were claiming $5 million in lost royalties, advances, guarantees, licensing fees, and Nesmith's personal financial pledge of $2 million in the initial deal. Pacific Arts countersued PBS for breach of contract, intentional misrepresentation, negligent misrepresentation, intentional concealment, fraud, and contractual interference.

Anticipating a lengthy legal fight, Nesmith was forced to cease Pacific Arts video operations. PBS was willing to take on more risk to get higher video revenue. It partnered with Turner Home Entertainment in a distribution fee deal for marketing, selling, and operational services. PBS was confident their full slate of programing would generate significantly more profits. This was a risky assumption as the new deal structure made PBS more vulnerable to a weak release schedule, underperforming content, and inventory returns.

The lawsuit continued to progress when in 1997 Warner Bros. bought New Line Cinema and Turner Broadcasting, which included the PBS video distribution rights. The PBS versus Pacific Arts lawsuit went to Federal court in February 1999. The jury unanimously awarding $40 million to Pacific Arts and $5 million to Nesmith personally from the plaintiffs. Pacific Arts was required to pay licensing royalties of $1.2 million to Ken Burns' company for *Civil War*, $230,000 to WGBH, and $130,000 to WNET.

Ken Burns Baseball (2000) and *Jazz* (2001) DVD releases were commercially successful for PBS and WBHE; however, there were no big commercial documentaries on the production slate beyond 2001.

Negotiating a New Distribution Agreement

The PBS–WBHE distribution deal was expiring in 2004, and we had concerns with continuing the relationship. First, PBS was looking to reduce the distribution fee to a below market level. Second, the extensive amount of WBHE management time needed to make PBS executives satisfied was problematic. We did all the business planning and retail execution, while they exercised their contractual approval rights of all aspects of their releases. PBS had unrealistic expectations for their content performance. Their attitude and workload expectation was like being on the PBS staff. Third, we wanted more broadly appealing programing, but PBS had little influence on their network of content producers. The thought of receiving a lower fee for more management time and fewer commercial hits was problematic.

We set a walkaway target distribution fee at slightly below-market level at 11 percent and offset the risk with a roll-over clause that automatically extended the deal if WB predetermined financial targets were not achieved. We expected the competition for the PBS rights would come from the smaller studios: Paramount, Sony, and Lionsgate. Another potential problem was a key WBHE senior executive left to become the president of Paramount Home Entertainment during the negotiations.

PBS seemed accepting of the 11 percent distribution fee offer. They invited our staff to Washington DC to finalize the deal and work on future plans. Believing this was a positive sign, I informed Warner Bros. management the deal would be signed over the next couple of days. Six of us flew cross-country and picked up the tab for a large dinner with PBS management. We had reserved a meeting room at the Four Seasons Hotel for an all-day work session, showing our commitment to work together and get a deal done the next day.

The next morning, the PBS Home Entertainment VP started the meeting with an announcement thanking us for the many years of a successful partnership; however, the market had changed and so must PBS. She informed the crowded meeting room that PBS agreed to terms last night with Paramount for a significantly lower distribution fee. Industry sources pegged the fee at under 10 percent. We sat in disbelief as the PBS VP and staffers quickly left the room, leaving us again with the tab for the room and breakfast!

It is a good management practice to provide a document of record when a business negotiation goes poorly. We let the embarrassment sink in as we dug through the rubble of the failed negotiation. We took the rest of the day to conduct a negotiation performance review.

As the day progressed, our feelings evolved from embarrassment to regret to a sense of relief. It was my responsibility for underestimating the competition for high-quality programing in a growing market. I should have expected the new president of Paramount Home Entertainment would go after the PBS deal to make an early impression with his management.

Unfortunately for Paramount, the five-year release schedule had no commercial Ken Burns documentaries. Dealing with the unrealistic demands of the high maintenance PBS management was an expensive soft cost. We were not going to distribute independent content for a single-digit distribution fee. We avoided losing millions of dollars on a below-market deal. The only real loss was to our self-esteem for flying cross-country only to get rejected.

Lessons Learned From PBS

- Establish financial targets before the negotiation to minimize emotions and walkaway when projections are below your target.
- Avoid organizations with negotiation red flags: unrealistic growth targets, tight cash flow, demanding leadership, matrix organization structure, or high employee turnover.
- Do not inform management of an optimistic outcome before a deal is signed—especially with difficult and untrustworthy partners.
- Never fly cross-country without a signed contract!

BBC

The BBC is a prestigious brand with a small but loyal domestic following. Every few years, the BBC would produce an original hit program, such as *Planet Earth*, that had the potential to pay for the entire deal. The BBC–WBHE agreement was one of the first video distribution deals in the emerging video market of the early 1990s. The uncertainty of the market necessitated a complex deal to protect each side's upside and downside. The five-year deal was the most collaborative of any of our negotiations.

The hybrid agreement consisted of both royalty and distribution fees with shared revenues and profits. The contract contained numerous consultations and approval rights as well as mutual options for extensions and exits. Both sides were willing to give easy outs to ensure neither side committed too early to a bad deal. Mutual trust was established early due to two conditions: the original WBHE lead negotiator was a dual U.S. and British citizen. Additionally, the BBC America and Time Warner headquarters were in close proximity to each other in mid-town Manhattan. The BBC–WBHE video distribution deal has lasted through three decades.

Lessons Learned From BBC Negotiations

- Contingency clauses are warranted when there is uncertainty in the market and product performance.
- Integrity and trust are essential negotiating traits in an emerging or volatile market.
- Matching the culture of the other side provides a competitive advantage in a negotiation.

National Geographic

National Geographic video distribution came to WBHE in the 1990s through their deal with Warner Bros. TV. Their strong brand name and action/science-based documentary programing made them a valued partner. By 2002, Nat Geo was going through a major reorganization in an attempt to better exploit the evolving entertainment market. They established a new theatrical acquisition team to pursue movies whose content fit the brand. Producing and acquiring theatrical movies is always a risky endeavor, but the growing DVD business provided an ample safety net.

When it was time for the contract renewal, Nat Geo wanted a market rate 15 percent distribution fee and a 2 percent marketing allowance to monetize their brand name. Nat Geo believed their documentaries outperformed unbranded documentaries and wanted to be paid a premium. WBHE agreed to pay a 2 percent marketing rebate based on retail net revenue; however, Nat Geo insisted their theatrical box office revenue be included in the formula.

The Warner Bros. theatrical division did not want to set a precedent and pay a marketing fee, so WBHE would fund the 2 percent marketing fee on all revenues to get the deal done. I viewed this as a *lottery ticket clause* because Nat Geo rarely had a theatrical release, let alone one with significant box office. Paying the rebate would give me a significant influence on the theatrical-home entertainment window. I wanted a good working relationship with Nat Geo and did not want to be a *difficult* negotiator with a long-time partner. The rebate appeared to be an easy *give* to close the deal.

In 2005, Nat Geo acquired the worldwide rights for a theatrical documentary at the Sundance Film Festival called, *March of the Penguins,* a French production about the lives of Arctic penguins with first person voiceovers by French actors.

Warner Bros. negotiated with Nat Geo for the domestic theatrical distribution rights, beating out Disney, which won the international rights. At the suggestion of Warner Bros. creative executives, Nat Geo changed the U.S. narration to be more traditional documentary third-person-style voiceover and hired Morgan Freeman to perform it. Warner Bros theatrical executed a platform release strategy starting with a small number of theaters in the United States and Canada. The expectations on both sides were to build awareness slowly, and if successful, expand the number of theaters to match demand. If the plan failed to generate a breakeven target box office, the residual awareness would benefit from a quick release to the home entertainment market. But then something magical occurred…

The U.S. and Canadian audiences loved the penguins! The movie was a breakout hit and eventually expanded to nearly 2,000 theaters grossing $77 million in domestic box office and $40 million in DVD revenue. The friendly gesture to include theatrical box office in the 2 percent marketing allowance formula cost WBHE an incremental $2.34 million.

Good gestures do get rewarded. The *March of the Penguins* generated enormous consumer appeal for penguins. The following year, Warner Bros. released an animated penguin film where it benefited from the *penguin halo. Happy Feet* was a critical and commercial hit, receiving a best animated picture Academy Award and generating $384 million in worldwide box office and over $200 million in DVD revenue.

Lessons Learned From Nat Geo

- Ensure that contract terms align with both sides go-to-market strategy and operational goals.
- In multiparty negotiations, you may have to compromise for the benefit of the overall deal.
- Equitable negotiations have both sides participating proportionately in the upside and the downside.

CHAPTER 15

Negotiating
Celebrity Content

Tiger, Oprah, Martha, and the Twins

With the sports and cable TV content locked up, we targeted market segments with appeal beyond the young male DVD fan base. Our analysis revealed opportunities with celebrity-driven content because of two market factors: a loyal fan base and the ability to promote their DVD releases throughout the year. Fans have an insatiable desire for their favorite celebrities' knowledge, skills, and lifestyle. The key to these negotiations is understanding the motivations of the celebrities and their desire to make the content successful.

Our content strategy was to produce a *Best of Celebrity* series in a high-price DVD box set. The distribution strategy was to acquire enough programing to create scale with a branded celebrity retail section. We evaluated all the talk shows and their hosts to determine which had the highest popularity and best content fit for DVD. Talk shows have a content challenge with their limited repeatable subject matter—the key motivating factor for buying a DVD. The two most highly rated shows were Oprah Winfrey and Martha Stewart. Each show had a popular personality, content depth, and the vehicle to promote the DVD.

With only two viable talk shows, we expanded our search to celebrity athletes in nonteam sports. With athletes, we wanted to produce compelling biographical documentaries with career highlights and playing lessons. At the top of our list was Tiger Woods.

The *Best of Celebrity* strategy had a few challenges. First, the negotiations were expected to be difficult because the celebrities' management were known to be tough negotiators. Second, the celebrities had reputations of being highly demanding of their staffs. A lot of WBHE time and resources would be required to produce content to their standards and achieve a satisfactory financial return. Third, *Best of Celebrity* initiative could be overly time-consuming and take away focus from our other established special interest content partners. Having to share fixed resources with unproven content partners was a risk. Fourth, my personal interest in this project, specifically Tiger Woods, could be perceived as a vanity project. Executives have been known to set up *self-interest* projects to have a personal relationship with the star. WB management would ask if my motivation to do the deal was to meet Tiger. My defense was having a portfolio of celebrities, including those targeted at female and teen audiences, justified my pursuit of the celebrity-branded strategy beyond Tiger.

The WBHE president eventually gave a *little yes* to move forward with the *Best of Celebrity* project. A *little yes* is a reluctant approval that turns into an "I told you so" if the project fails. What swayed him were these projects established direct access to three global celebrities who potentially could do a movie or tv show with Warner Bros. in the future. Their DVD deals would increase the WBHE president's stature in the Time Warner executive suite. When getting management approval, pointing out how it would benefit them professionally is a good negotiation tactic.

Tiger Woods Negotiation

Tiger Woods was at the height of his popularity in the early 2000s. A DVD release had the potential to bridge our retail sports presence to launch the *Best of Celebrity* project. The product concept, the *Ultimate Tiger Woods DVD*, would go beyond our previously released professional sports teams *Ultimate* biographies. *The Ultimate Tiger Woods* three-DVD box set would include highlights from his major tournament wins, his greatest shots with his commentary, and a new technology, an interactive instructional segment.

Many of my colleagues believed golf is too boring a sport, and the 55+ demographic was not a fit for DVD. I believed Tiger transcended golf and appealed to a broader demographic of 18 to 54. He was a global star, and the new interactive concept would generate publicity for the DVD format. Having internal doubters requires extra time and analysis to support revenue projections and quantify an acceptable level of risk.

I received approval to begin the *Best of Celebrity* project with Tiger Woods in the beginning of 2003. We sent Tiger's agent, Mark Steinberg a treatment of the concept along with a brief deal structure without financials. The key to the project was getting Tiger's commitment, especially his influence to acquire footage from third parties. We estimated the need for 40 hours of Tiger's time. The optimal release timing was to coincide with *The Masters* golf tournament, the first major of the golf season, in April 2004. Steinberg responded that he liked the idea and would discuss it with Tiger, but there was no commitment to our timetable. Our firm deadline created an initial negotiation edge for Steinberg.

A month later, Steinberg called me on the Sunday night before the Thursday start of the 2003 Masters tournament. Tiger liked the concept and wanted to discuss it in more detail. Tiger's schedule was booked solid through July; however, he had 15 minutes available on Tuesday at 8:00 a.m. at Augusta National Golf Course. This would require a flight to Atlanta, GA, and a three-hour drive to Augusta.

Despite the critical need to get started, I declined to attend for three reasons. First, it would take a minimum of three days out of the office to meet with Tiger and Steinberg. My absence would increase my president's perception I was doing this deal for personal gain to meet Tiger at the famed Augusta National Golf Club. Second, an offer to meet across the country on a ridiculous short notice was a negotiation tactic by Steinberg to test my level of interest. You don't get to be Tiger's agent without some serious negotiating skills. I was going to learn from this challenge regardless of the outcome. Third, my response needed to position WBHE bringing more value to the deal. Tiger should come to Warner Bros. Whichever party needs the other the more, is at a negotiation disadvantage. Another edge to Steinberg.

Steinberg and I had numerous calls throughout the May–August 2003 golf season refining the product concept, the deal terms, and our expectations of Tiger's participation with the production and promoting the release. Steinberg wanted a level of detail in our discussions that would require a nondisclosure agreement (NDA). After all our discussions, I realized my mistake. I had given him enough information to take the product concept and deal terms to another studio to get a better offer. Having success with the NFL, NBA, NHL, and WCW, I did not think any other studio could match our product development and market strength. With the negotiation edge clearly with them, I was pulled into having a compromise strategy.

By the end of summer, there was no progress. I realized we could not make our optimal release date. This project was going to be the kind of deal that takes years to complete. Without the time pressure of a release date, I went back to my negotiation fundamentals and sent an NDA. Steinberg expressed interest to sign it, but Tiger still had a few issues with the product concept. Steinberg asked for a fully written product concept description and a short form deal memo. This behavior confirmed to me they were engaged with another studio.

I requested a signed NDA before we would send the product details and deal memo. Steinberg said he was comfortable signing an NDA; however, over the next two weeks, he made multiple credible excuses why the NDA wasn't signed yet. The mark of a good negotiator is having credible excuses! I reached out to my industry connections trying to find out which studio was doing a Tiger Woods deal. Apparently, there was some kind of agreement between Tiger and the Disney Cruise Lines.

I still believed we would get the deal because the Disney content strategy focused on big IP movies and TV shows with high licensing revenue for their theme parks and consumer products businesses. For Disney, the Tiger Woods DVD is off strategy and the type of outside project that causes distraction.

I scheduled a meeting with Steinberg and Tiger during his charity tournament at Sherwood Country Club in Thousand Oaks, California, only 30 miles from Warner Bros. studio. Tiger agreeing to meet at the studio gave me optimism the deal was finally going to get done. Then just days before the meeting and the tourney, Steinberg informed me Disney was going to do the Tiger Woods DVD due to his sponsorship deal with the Disney cruise lines.

I was not surprised by the call confirming we were a stalking horse. My assumption how this happened was that after our initial discussions, Steinberg told Disney they should do a DVD box set for Tiger. Disney corporate told the home entertainment division to produce and release a *Tiger Woods DVD* to keep him happy, but don't lose money. Studios reluctantly produce vanity projects to prevent their *assets* from making money for other studios.

The Disney *Tiger Woods DVD* box set was a low-cost production made with footage from old interviews, highlights, and clinic appearances. With minimal Disney support, Tiger had little financial and creative incentives to promote the DVD release in November 2004. With low production value and consumer awareness, the Disney *Tiger Woods DVD* received mediocre reviews (3.8 out of 5) and had modest sales.

Lessons Learned From Tiger

- Get to the decision maker early in the negotiation to sell your capabilities and determine their interest.
- If the key person is too busy to meet with you, they will be too busy to participate in the production or other contract performances.
- Overcoming internal objections requires robust analytics to support revenue projections and quantify an acceptable level of risk.
- Expect your deal is being shopped if there is hesitation in signing the NDA.

Oprah Winfrey/Harpo Productions Negotiation

There is a symbiotic relationship with electronic devices and content. For DVD sales to continue to grow, hardware prices needed to be lower and content needed to appeal to females. By 2004, DVD hardware expanded to the mainstream households when prices dipped below the $300 price point. Now the DVD households were ready for content targeting females 25 to 44 years old. Our priority was content with the highest and most loyal female viewership, *The Oprah Winfrey Show*.

Oprah produced her show through her production company, Harpo Productions, which was distributed by Paramount Television. We wanted Oprah to produce and promote a DVD of her show's best segments to influence females to buy another DVD player for the house. This would grow the DVD player installed base. Being the market leader with a 35 percent share, WBHE could expect incremental revenue from every new DVD household. This growth strategy is known as *a rising tide lifts all boats*.

We met with the president of Harpo Productions, who thought *The Best of Oprah* DVD concept was a feasible production with good commercial appeal. The key component in the deal was the low clip licensing fees as Oprah owns her show. The main production costs would be editing and marketing. We viewed the project as a low risk–moderate reward. It is beneficial in any negotiation when both parties have similar expectations for the potential of the project.

Oprah and Harpo Productions knew exactly what to do and how they were going to do it. They asked for a distribution fee deal where Harpo would pay WBHE a fee to distribute and market the DVD globally. WBHE would advance the marketing funds and deduct the funds, the minimum guaranty and distribution fee from collected net revenue for managing the day-to-day business with worldwide retailers. This structure would enable Oprah to control all aspects of the project while assuming most of the financial risk and upside. By owning the production, Harpo could set their production and release schedule to Oprah's availability.

Our initial offer was a small advance and 15 percent distribution fee, which was the market rate for independent content distribution. Harpo Productions was well funded, so cash flow was not an issue. They wanted a distribution partner with a global reach and strong marketing to expand the Oprah brand. If there was resistance on the advance or fee terms, our financial projections allowed us to go to a $1 million advance and a 12 percent fee. We knew our main competition would be Paramount Home Entertainment due to the Paramount–Harpo TV deal. Another serious competitor would be Sony whose lucrative international TV deal would be attractive to Oprah's global interests.

We believe we had the negotiation edge versus the competition. First was the scale of the WBHE dedicated resources in marketing, distribution, operations, and financial accounting. Second, our ability to maximize Oprah's retail presence is proven by our sports and documentary sections. Third, our industry leading global reach would generate the most worldwide exposure. Smaller studios, such as Paramount, license their content in many of the international territories to other studios and could not directly manage the business. Another advantage was Oprah's fondness for Warner Bros., which gave her a start in the movie industry by casting her in the film, *THE COLOR PURPLE.*

Harpo Productions TV distribution deal with Paramount was an unavoidable risk as they could easily take the *Best of Oprah* concept. Oprah could leverage Paramount to get whatever they wanted without negotiating. Enhancing the risk was the new Paramount Home Entertainment president would be motivated to gain favor with Oprah and her company executives. This is another example of a studio not wanting talent to leak to another studio. You don't want to be the Paramount executive who let an Oprah project go to another studio. The decision for Paramount was simple: how much time and money was needed to keep Oprah happy with this project? The answer was whatever Oprah wanted it to be.

Oprah was not available to meet with us any time soon, which raised a red flag. When the owner cannot meet with you, the deal value is too low or someone else is getting the deal. After my Tiger Woods and PBS lessons, I assumed we were the stalking horse in this situation. The upside to our effort to pursue Oprah was that Paramount, with limited resources, would need to spend time and money on this project. Hopefully it would weaken them from competing with us for other independent content. This competitive strategy motivated us to see the negotiation to its eventual outcome. We were not surprised when Oprah signed a single-digit distribution fee deal with Paramount Home Entertainment.

Lessons Learned From Oprah Winfrey/Harpo Productions Negotiations

- There is little chance of getting an agreement in a competitive negotiation without getting a face-to-face meeting with the ultimate decision maker.
- A good competitive strategy is to drain the resources of your competitor by leading them into a difficult deal.
- When the owner cannot meet with you, the deal value is too low or someone else is getting the deal.

Martha Stewart Living Omni (MSLO) Negotiation

In March 2005, Martha Stewart was getting out of prison having served her five-month incarceration. She had been convicted of a $40,000 securities fraud/insider trading crime. We were curious if Ms. Stewart and her company, Martha Stewart Living Omni (MSLO) could regain her immense popularity and fan base. She had the potential to attract a new female demographic to DVD. There was no precedent for a revenue forecast of a celebrity coming out of prison and relaunching a high-end entertainment and merchandise business. This meduim-risk–low reward proposition would need safeguards to mitigate the downside.

I contacted her company, expecting a collaborative negotiation. We met with the president of the MSLO media company to discuss their plans to relaunch the brand and our plans for a *Best of Martha Stewart* DVD line produced from her favorite TV show segments. Although we were only small parts in each other's plans, both sides had realistic expectations on the project.

MSLO relaunch plans included building the *Martha Stewart Living* brand through the TV show, multiple cooking and housekeeping handbooks, her signature soft goods line in K-Mart and Sears, a Macy's housewares line, a flooring line, a partnership with Gallo wines, and her own radio show on Sirius Satellite Radio. Ms. Stewart and her organization were determined to grow her business back to the levels prior to her legal troubles. Failure was not an option for them. There were multiple lines of products to create and retail relationships to repair. Ms. Stewart recognized *The Best of Martha Stewart* DVDs could help support MSLO relaunch by expanding her brand name into a new retail channels. There were numerous plans to be coordinated, and they wanted a deal now.

Our critical deal term was Ms. Stewart's time and creativity as she was stretched in so many directions. We needed her to contractually agree to an amount of creative development time. I learned from my previous missteps to request an NDA to ensure confidentiality of our product strategy. They signed it immediately after our first meeting as both parties felt the time urgency of the brand relaunch.

Ms. Stewart was fully engaged in the negotiations, which had a positive and negative impact for us. She wanted to meet our group in NYC. For the meeting, she had prepared the best meeting lunch ever! True to her brand and reputation, everything was orderly, comfortable, and in good taste. This was a positive sign of her commitment and being able to work with her organization. She immediately gave us her two objectives for the project. The first was a need for a significant cash advance. Going to prison reduced many of her revenue streams. Most performance contracts have a moral turpitude clause, meaning the contract is suspended if one party does something wrong like committing a felony. Ours would include this protection in case of additional legal difficulties.

Second, she wanted her DVD to get maximum retail exposure to support her brand relaunch plans, especially in grocery chains where she only had magazine distribution. Martha Stewart is a savvy businessperson. She understood the retail consumer goods business and its 100 percent returns capability, so if her DVD did not sell, the unsold units could create a large financial expense. She was also cognizant of the limits on her availability and the creative production process. WBHE would produce the content with her creative approval.

We had the negotiation edge by knowing her brand relaunch deadline and the need for a cash advance. We quickly settled on a royalty structure with a low rate, but a generous cash advance, which we would recoup over a three-year deal. Importantly, WBHE would own the DVD inventory, which gave us pricing flexibility if the initial sales were below expectations. By giving her an appropriate level of cash up front, we ensured her involvement for creating content and publicity. We compromised on the other terms as we didn't want to over negotiate with the founder and creator of the content. With cooperation on both sides, the first DVD was launched within nine months and was a moderate success for each party.

Lessons Learned From Martha Stewart Negotiations

- The traits of the leader of an organization establish the organization culture.
- Knowing the needs of the decision maker upfront will help you select the right strategy.
- The high-profile owner/founder will overvalue themselves and be offended if you offer less than their self-perception.
- If the owner/founder attends the negotiation, the expectation is to reach an agreement by the end of the meeting.
- If the deal doesn't get completed in the presence of the owner, the probability of closing will be much lower in subsequent meetings.

Dualstar Contract Extension Negotiation

Another celebrity opportunity was to extend our relationship with Mary Kate and Ashley Olsen. There were no bigger child stars in the 1990s than Mary Kate and Ashley Olsen. The Olsen Twins starred in the Warner Bros. TV series, *Full House* in 1987–1995. They had formed their own production and merchandising company called Dualstar. WBHE signed them in 1992 to distribute made-for-video movies targeted at girls 8 to 11 years. Dualstar produced the content and paid WBHE a fee to distribute 13 *Mary Kate & Ashley* direct-to-video films from 1992 to 2002. The *Mary Kate & Ashley* branded merchandise was not part of the WBHE agreement. These direct-to-video movies and licensed merchandise made them millionaires before their eighth birthday.

Their 10-year distribution agreement with WBHE was expiring in 2002. They were no longer juveniles and were looking to do projects beyond direct-to-video kid movies.

Now 16 years old, the Olsen twins' personal interests and tastes were maturing. Dualstar had a tough, hands-on manager who controlled all contact with the twins. Our discussions with the manager indicated Mary Kate and Ashley wanted to produce and act in theatrically released movies with young adult content. They also wanted to upgrade their kids merchandise to a young adult fashion line.

The contract extension would be for theatrically released movies to be distributed by Warner Bros. theatrical division. The themes would be teenage issues such as dating and post high-school life. The new deal would be a high-risk/high-reward proposition. The risk was the teen-themed content could alienate mothers and their young girl fan base. The reward would be attracting the female fans *aging-up* and a new demographic of males 16 to 21 years of age—the largest movie going demographic. The twins wanted the new movies to drive sales of their new young adult fashions.

Three Warner Bros. divisions wanted to do business with Dualstar: theatrical, home entertainment, and licensing. When there are many points of interest dealing within a multidivisional corporation, one division takes the lead. It is usually the one who *owns the relationship* or the highest revenue potential. Home entertainment took the lead as we had the relationship with the manager and the highest revenue from the *Mary Kate & Ashley* DVD catalog. WBHE liked the idea of delivering the next big movie franchise to the studio and increasing the value of the *Mary Kate & Ashley* video library. WBHE was paying the advance for the deal, so the theatrical division essentially was getting *free* movies. This situation is the reverse of the usual studio theatrical-home entertainment relationship where theatrical takes the early financial risk and home entertainment benefits from the *free* movies. WB licensing wanted to distribute the Dualstar merchandise but did not want to insert themselves into the negotiation.

Dualstar had the negotiation edge and utilized a *competitive strategy* as it owned their DVD library content and could get a new distribution deal with any other studio. It is a common industry practice for one studio to outbid the original studio when contracts are expiring. You either steal the talent or you make your competitor overpay to keep their talent. We did a similar maneuver by getting the Disney-based producers of *Air Bud* movies to produce direct-to-video movies for WBHE. They created the successful *Most Valuable Primate* (MVP) franchise of a skateboarding chimpanzee.

Two WBHE executives had a personal relationship with the Dualstar manager, so they ran lead on the negotiations. My involvement in the negotiations was on a need-to-know basis. I reluctantly accepted a stakeholder role despite having the responsibility to deliver the results of the new deal. They wanted to utilize a *collaborative strategy* but eventually turned into a *compromise strategy*. One of the WBHE executives socialized with the Dualstar manager and had visited the set of the direct-to-video movies as a guest of the production. The negotiations were moving quickly with little transparency. The tone of the negotiation was congenial as everyone assumed the new movie was going to be a success.

The ten-year proposed deal extension had both short-term and long-term risk. The short-term risk was that if the movie failed in the theatrical window, it meant that young adults were not willing to accept the twins as peers. There would be further financial losses in the home entertainment window as older teens would not buy the new movie DVD. The long-term risk was the value of the DVD movie catalog would plummet as moms would stop buying the DVDs for their young daughters.

Another negotiating error was the lack of direct access to Mary Kate and Ashley Olsen to determine what they were really thinking. We were ready to pay them an eight-figure deal but did not know their state of mind. Compounding the situation, all three WB divisions thought they were doing the other division a business favor by having a new deal. Having favors as an upside can lead to a bad deal.

In risky situations, it is prudent to have an early exit clause in the contract. This would give either side an *out* if the movie did not work or the twins wanted to pursue something else. A lot can change when the contract principals go from 16-year-olds to 26-year-olds. And a lot did…

With Disney circling, the deal was quickly negotiated to provide Dualstar marketing and distribution services along with a multimillion-dollar advance. The movie, *In a New York Minute*, was a rushed $30 million production and opened wide in over 3,000 theaters domestically. It was a critical and box office failure, generating only U.S. $15 million in domestic box office and U.S.$7 million internationally. Siskel & Ebert gave it "two thumbs down" and IMDB rated it 5 out of 10 stars. The subsequent DVD release had similarly poor results.

Mary Kate and Ashley Olson were 18 years old when the movie was released. With the failure, they decided to leave the movie business to attend New York University and start another fashion business. There were no more films or TV programs as Dualstar went into dormancy. Although we would have been severely criticized in the industry at the time, it may have been better to let Disney sign the twins.

Lessons Learned From Dualstar Negotiation

- Don't shortcut your negotiation process regardless of relationships. Once you lose the discipline, you will eventually make a bad deal.
- Always have direct communication with the key assets or performers in the contract. They will reveal their true intentions over time, especially if you get them one-on-one in a social setting.
- Having managers and agents as go-betweens introduces a lot of self-dealing, half-truths, and misinformation.
- Always negotiate with a united front. Do not allow the other side to divide and conquer.

CHAPTER 16

Negotiating Versus Industry Disruptors

How Netflix and Redbox Beat the Studios

The Launch of DVD

By the late 1990s, Blockbuster was the leading home entertainment entity annually buying over $1.6 billion worth of videos from the major studios and independent production companies. Their buying power was so dominant that their order could make or break a movie's profitability. Blockbuster knew they had the negotiation edge and behaved as the market bully using competitive strategies in their negotiations. However, the launch of DVD enabled studios to expand their revenue base with new retailers such as Wal-Mart, Target, Best Buy, and Amazon. Studios expanded distribution across various types of retailers, such as grocery stores and airports, which decreased the market dominance of Blockbuster.

The studios wanted DVD to be a transactional consumer *ownership* model as this was more profitable than sharing rental revenue with video stores. A DVD disc, packaging and shipping expenses costs about $1. The studio's new release DVD price to retailers was around $15, making it the studio's most profitable individual transaction of a movie's lifecycle. By comparison, the studio generally makes about $4.50 on a theatrical ticket price of $10. The studios wanted consumers to become DVD collectors and have a sense of pride owning a movie library. This was a superior consumer experience to watching outdated movies on subscription channels HBO and Cinemax. The premium cable channels responded by producing low-budget original content to differentiate their market position and maintain their subscriber base. This original content strategy was only moderately successful; however, it would change the industry a decade later with Netflix.

Netflix Disruption

DVD enabled Netflix to start as a mail order subscription DVD rental business in 1997. The size and shape of the DVD discs made their business model feasible versus the large bulky VHS cassette tapes. Their consumer offering was an inexpensive alternative to buying DVDs with the added convenience of ordering online. With Netflix, you were able to watch any movie you wanted without having to go back and forth to a video store and no late fees. Perhaps their greatest attribute was the ease of searching for your favorite movies on their website. They developed a highly effective curation software that analyzed your viewing history and prompted you to preorder similar upcoming movies. Despite the many consumer-friendly innovations, the studios did not view the Netflix subscription model as a threat to their high-margin transactional business.

Blockbuster Failed Negotiations

Warner Bros. supported Netflix with favorable DVD content deals to be a viable competitor to Blockbuster. There were numerous times in the Netflix's first five years where their cash flow was tight, and the studios helped with extended credit and development funds. It has been well documented that during these times, Netflix reached out to Blockbuster to be acquired. Blockbuster was not interested because they were launching their own direct mail DVD rental club. The Blockbuster Franchisee Stores opposed the DVD-by-mail initiative because of its disruption to their in-store traffic. The internally powerful Blockbuster Franchisee Owners believed Blockbuster Online was keeping their customers out of their stores and wanted corporate to shut it down. Blockbuster ignored the competitive strategy to acquire a small, but growing competitor to increase its consumer base and mitigate competitive in-roads.

Although competitive with Netflix for years, Blockbuster Online was eventually shut down in 2007. Blockbuster management's inability to collaboratively negotiate with the stakeholder franchisees created one of the biggest corporate mistakes in the history of U.S. business.

The Netflix Edge: Strategy Evolution

The Netflix leadership evolved their business strategies without revealing their future intentions during collaborative negotiations with the studios. They initially positioned themselves as a viable competitor to Block-buster and helped the studios neutralize the market-dominating rental chain. Netflix grew their importance to the studios by paying hundreds of millions of dollars to acquire studio's new releases and library DVDs. The revenue more than offset the studio's declining television syndication deals. The studios reluctantly accepted Netflix revenue despite the perceived cannibalization of the more profitable retail DVD consumer sales. The studios increased their support by annually paying millions of dollars in development funds to finetune Netflix's curation software and consumer marketing. The studios first error was failing to require viewing data to monitor the Netflix growth and track the cannibalizing the studio's movie, DVD, and video on demand (VOD) transactional businesses.

Netflix Ultimate Goal

In 2007, Netflix continued to increase their value to the studios by paying digital streaming licensing fees for movies and TV shows. This new business competed directly with premium pay TV entities HBO and Showtime. The studios were happy with the new digital licensing revenue, except for Warner Bros., who was conflicted supporting a direct competitor to its sister division HBO. Netflix was able to negotiate the license for a relatively small fee because they were just starting up. The studios repeated their negotiating error by not requiring Netflix to report digital viewing data. Over time, this lack of transparency enabled Netflix to keep the digital payments low and prevented the studios from reacting to the Netflix growth until it was too late.

2010 was the pivotal year in the relationship between Netflix and the six major movie studios. Netflix became a dominant player in the entertainment industry with subscription rental DVD and digital stream-ing. All the video rental chains were now closed and Netflix achieved subscriber scale with HBO and Showtime.

Netflix Versus Warner Bros. Negotiation Showdown

Warner Bros. CEO Kevin Tsujihara was in a difficult spot. Negotiating a successful Netflix deal extension would provide the studio significant revenue growth over the next three years. However, it would make HBO's biggest competitor even stronger. Netflix gained the edge by negotiat-ing three separate content deals with WB: rental DVD, streaming movie, and streaming television. WBHE negotiated their DVD deal, WB Dig-ital Distribution negotiated their movie digital deal, and WB Television Distribution negotiated their TV digital deal.

Tsujihara realized the disadvantage and stepped in as the WB lead negotiator. He held the negotiations in his office at a round table to set a casual and friendly environment. The attendees were Tsujihara, the WB distribution head, and me across from Netflix CEO Reed Hastings and head of content Ted Sarandos. Having the distribution head and myself in the meeting was to position the new deal as being led by DVD with the digital pieces as add-ons. Tsujihara, understanding both the cannibaliza-tion of DVD sales and being a competitor to HBO, wanted to put Netflix on the defensive. He opened by tossing a *negotiation grenade* stating WB did not like Netflix's subscription model because it was not good for the studio or the industry. The strength of the movie revenue comes from transactions where consumers pay for each viewing of the content: movie tickets, DVD sales, and transactional VOD. With Netflix growth, sub-scriptions became the preferred consumer payment for content. Theaters, DVD retailers, and cable companies were now lower preferences for con-sumers. This trend had an unfavorable impact on studio profit margins.

The Netflix negotiation strategy was to *collaborate* and *compromise* so as not to appear as a threat. They would continue to pay WBHE a large sum for DVD revenue share deal, which offset the shortfall from the collapse of the video store rental business. Netflix reinforced that their streaming launch was competing with cable and satellite companies, not retailers and premium pay TV (HBO). Digital piracy was another threat that Netflix was helping the studios mitigate. Lastly, Netflix pointed to the main threat to the studios was free user-generated content (UGC) and DVRs. Their research showed these relatively new technologies were now the first choice for content in most households.

Netflix ability to position themselves as *collaborative* partners fighting for the greater good of the industry diffused Warner Bros. initial *competitive* position. Netflix used a *compromise strategy* by agreeing to pay Warner Bros. what they wanted for DVD and streaming rights. Hastings was clever to not reveal his vision of digital dominance through superior customer content curation and original programing. He let the studios believe streaming was only a convenience to get consumers to sign up and maintain a Netflix DVD subscription. The meeting ended with Warner Bros. believing Netflix would be a trusted partner by paying WB more money with each new business they launched. Publicly, the studios were not supportive of the Netflix business model, but they continued to take multiple Netflix checks and provide them a steady flow of content … until it was too late.

Netflix Becomes a Competitor

Netflix shifted to a hybrid *competitive* and *collaborative* strategy when they revealed their original programing launch in 2012. The studios believed Netflix created a fourth revenue stream for them by renting sound stages, editing equipment, and other production services to produce their original content. There was little concern with Netflix *competing* with the studios for creative talent.

When asked at the time if HBO considered Netflix a threat, Time Warner CEO Jeff Bewkes replied, "It's a little bit like, is the Albanian army going to take over the world? I don't think so." This was one of the biggest competitive threat assessment errors in U.S. business history.

The studios continued to view Netflix as outsiders who would eventually spend themselves into a cash flow problem like most new production companies. The best-case scenario was Netflix would have low to moderate success producing selective content like HBO and Showtime. At worst, they would lose money and eventually be forced to cut back on production. The first content released by Netflix was *Lillehammer*, which was critically panned but liked by a modest number of viewers. The second program, *House of Cards,* was expensive and risky. It paid off as the program turned into a multiple-season hit. In the next few years, Netflix would lead a content arms race, spending tens of billions, generating an immense change in the industry landscape.

Lessons Learned From Netflix Negotiations

- Keep the negotiation meetings small and in a friendly place to avoid the other side creating a grandstanding public posture or internal mob mentality.
- Keep calm when the meeting starts with a *grenade*: a challenging statement that puts you on the defensive. Let the *grenade thrower* fully explain their rationale. Remain positive with a friendly tone until you can deflect the aggression to a common enemy.
- Maintain a collaborative position by solving for the other side's main concern (e.g., incremental revenue growth).
- Reinforce the benefits you provide from being in business together. You may not be successful in this meeting; however, the goal is to be invited back.
- One side will often take short-term money over long-term vision.

Redbox Disruption

In 2002, the DVD format enabled another low-cost retailer to enter the market, Redbox, a DVD rental kiosk offering one-day rentals for $1. Redbox started inside select McDonalds stores before being purchased by Coinstar, a coin exchange vending machine company. Using the Coinstar in-store merchandising team, Redbox was able to expand into grocery, drug, and convenience stores. Redbox retail agreements were negotiated to share a small percentage of their rental revenue with retailers in exchange for prime front-of-store locations. Retailers liked the incremental revenue and the added benefit of the store traffic Redbox generated. Fridays and Saturdays were the highest rental pickup days, while Sundays and Mondays were the highest return days for the DVDs. Redbox and retailer contracts were *collaboratively negotiated* for the mutual benefits of this new low-priced entertainment business.

Studios were conflicted about the Redbox business model. They liked having a new revenue source as a replacement for Blockbuster and as a competitor to Netflix. Their concern was the potential Redbox cannibalization of the $15 DVD retail sale and $6 video on demand cable and satellite revenue. The prevailing wisdom was the better the movie, the higher the cannibalization. Studios tried to have it both ways by making it difficult by not selling directly to Redbox, who was forced to acquire DVDs from video wholesale distributors. The bigger studios Disney, Fox, Warner Bros., and Universal each took the hard position of not negotiating with Redbox. The smaller studios Sony, Paramount, and Lionsgate believed most of the rental revenue was incremental for their smaller movies, but they followed the industry leaders ... until there was a better opportunity.

Redbox filed a lawsuit against the studios based on the First Sale Doctrine, which allows anyone who buys a product to do with it as they please so long as it doesn't materially hurt the brand. The studios' legal position was Redbox's extremely low price was hurting the DVD brand. The studios had no urgency to resolve the disagreement as Redbox was a small business and not a major threat in the foreseeable future.

Down Economy Propels Redbox

In 2008, four related events occurred: the U.S. economy took a downturn, the launch of the new premium-priced Blu Ray Disc stalled, consumers started to rent more DVDs and Wal-Mart, the leading seller of DVDs, placed Redbox kiosks in the front of all 3,800 stores. These factors catapulted Redbox into a growth business the studios needed. The lawsuits were dropped, and the studios began to negotiate with Redbox to offset their DVD sales decline.

Redbox offered the studios revenue share output deals. For a minimum guaranteed upfront payment to the studios, Redbox would take predetermined quantities of every new release studio movie. The Redbox purchase requirement was based on a complex box office and genre formula. These revenue share deals enabled Redbox to pay a small upfront fee for each DVD ($1–$5) and split the $1 rental revenue after recoupment of the initial payment. The studios would receive about $.70 per rental transaction since the average Redbox consumer rental transaction was two nights.

Day and Date Versus Delayed Release Date Negotiations

Redbox began to offer studios very attractive terms for the ability to get DVDs at the same time as the retailers. The term was called *day and date*. The three smaller studios Sony, Paramount, and Lionsgate wanted day and date Redbox rental availability because their movie slate of lower box office films needed the revenue. The four big studios Disney, Warner, Fox, and Universal had larger movie slates and wanted less cannibalization, so they disadvantaged Redbox by having release dates delayed four to eight weeks after DVD retailers. The Redbox delayed payment terms were much lower as the rental activity was significantly less when delayed.

Redbox provided the kiosks with a consistently good selection of new movies by staggering the content offerings. Most consumers were unaware of the delays. If the kiosk did not have the movie the consumer wanted, there were many other new movies from which to choose. At only $1 per night, many consumers would rent multiple DVDs to ensure everyone at home was satisfied. Redbox became an industry growth vehicle, which created a negotiation edge. They had three negotiating strategies for the top seven movie studios: *Collaborative* with day and date, *compromise* with a four-week delay, and *compete* by buying indirectly at retail.

First-Mover Advantage Studios

Sony took the first-mover advantage in the Redbox content negotiations by agreeing to a seven-year, day and date, output deal. Redbox paid double the market-rate guarantee with an unlimited number of movies from Sony. The deal was extremely advantageous to Sony, given their movie slate was comprised of a couple of box office hits and dozens of small independent films. These independent acquisitions had little to no box office but rented relatively well compared to their box office performance.

Consumers preferred to rent smaller movies believing they were not worth paying $9 to see in theaters, $15 to own on DVD, or $6 to view on video on demand. Sony viewed Redbox DVD rental revenue as highly incremental and a necessity to reach their financial targets.

The unlimited output term would eventually harm Redbox the last year of the deal. A painful Redbox lesson was long-term deals in a volatile market need to have an *out clause* as one of the parties will get hurt toward the end of the deal.

Soon after the Redbox–Sony deal was announced, Paramount quickly agreed to a seven-year, day and date, Redbox output deal. The Paramount theatrical slate composition was similar to Sony's but with fewer small, independent movies. Redbox was able to negotiate slightly lower terms than Sony as Paramount was second to agree to terms.

With deal momentum in the market, Redbox was able to offset these two above-market content deals with a below-market, day and date, three-year deal with Lionsgate. The mini-major's movie slate box office was comprised of a few hits, but mostly acquired small independent movies. The Redbox rental revenue for independent movies could contributed 50 to 75 percent to the movie's total revenue. If Redbox did not buy these movies, many would be a financial loss for Lionsgate. Redbox had the negotiation edge and used it effectively to get their lowest cost deal in the market.

One Redbox downside to having direct deals with these studios was the elimination of the previously viewed DVD revenue. Redbox had developed a steady revenue stream selling used DVDs to distressed product wholesalers. The studios did not want previously viewed DVDs in the market as they were considered cannibalistic to their high margin DVD sales. The studio deals required Redbox to destroy the DVDs once their rental activity was over.

Four-Week Delay Studios

The following year, Warner Bros., Fox, and Universal, with annual box office value ranging from $1.3 to $1.9 billion, each negotiated output deals with Redbox. These studios agreed to a four-week holdback worth about half the revenue than the day and date studio agreements. Despite each receiving payment just under $100 million annually, all three studios continued to publicly denounce Redbox for hurting the movie industry with their low-price rental transactions. One studio's home entertainment president said, "Redbox is the cockroach of the industry. They eat away at us and we can't kill it." These studios behaved like the police chief in the movie, *Casablanca,* who was shocked that there was gambling in the establishment as he accepted his winnings.

The Disruptor Becomes Disrupted

Redbox had become the largest division of the public company, Outerwall. It had grown into a $1.6 billion DVD, Blu Ray and Video Game rental business with 35,000 U.S. locations and 41 million customers. The other two divisions were the coin exchange kiosks, Coinstar, and the fledgling used electronic device exchange kiosk, EcoATM. The company's financial strength was the robust cash flow generated from the coin exchanges and daily DVD rentals.

By 2014, the widespread availability of free digital content and acceptance of streaming movies changed the Redbox future. The DVD rental decline sent the Outerwall stock price tumbling and best described as a *falling knife.* Redbox began to implement severe cost savings programs, including numerous rounds of layoffs. These efforts could not fully offset the revenue declines. The biggest cost savings opportunity was the $600 million annual cost of content. Each of the six studio deals (no deal with Disney) were coming up for renewal in 2014 to 2016 and to survive, Redbox needed to negotiate significant cost reductions from all the studios. I was hired in August 2014, as Redbox head of content to lead the Redbox content negotiations against the studios. My 20 years with Warner Bros. leveled the playing field for Redbox negotiating content with the studios.

Upheaval Before the Battle

One can expect turmoil in the boardroom of any struggling company, but unforeseen internal changes increased the challenge of the 2015 to 2016 Redbox studio negotiations. In January 2015, the Outerwall CEO was fired. Then, the interim CEO was terminated after a few months. Many of the executives and key staff were either leaving for better jobs or victims of multiple rounds of layoffs. A third CEO was hired in August 2015, and he quickly fired the Redbox president. I was feeling like a test pilot trying to level off the out-of-control, spiraling-down jet. I tapped into my previous crisis experiences at Tylenol, Nabisco, and AOLTW. Follow company direction, focus on your performance, expand responsibilities, and good things will happen.

Redbox Negotiation Strategies Versus the Studios 2015 to 2016

The first Redbox negotiation strategy was to stagger each negotiation at the end of the studio's fiscal quarter or financial year. This timing puts pressure on the publicly held studios needing the guaranteed Redbox revenue to make their financial targets. On quarterly earnings calls, analysts and investors would ask the studios about their movie slates and the status of distribution agreements such as the Redbox output deal. Wall Street liked Redbox steady payments to the capital-intensive studio business. At the same time, Redbox would inform analysts which studio deals were being extended or going *out of deal*. The investment community was knowledgeable of the positive short-term financial impact to Redbox buying DVDs at retail. However, Wall Street prefers stable business conditions. As a public company, we needed to balance short-term leverage with long-term, stable studio relationships.

Redbox Negotiation Edge

Redbox had the negotiation edge due to a very effective workaround plan: the alternative method to source DVD content from retail. Redbox merchandisers visited each kiosk weekly. Their advanced software would direct them to the optimal route to purchase new release DVDs from Wal-Mart. These were often discounted to under $15, making the purchases financially better than having a direct studio deal. The merchandisers would remove the discs from the packages and insert them into 40,000 kiosks all within the first week of release. Eventually, the used DVDs were then sold to distress distributors for additional profit.

The Redbox organizational capacity maxed out at two studio work-arounds at a time. Having one negotiation per quarter enabled Redbox to leverage the workaround alternative scenario. The Redbox workaround plan caused studios financial and logistical difficulties and gave Redbox the early negotiation edge.

Another Redbox advantage was the importance in the first and second quarters of the calendar year when the studios are more reliant on revenues from Redbox. Redbox could hurt a studio's quarterly performance by not buying their movies. Being out of deal and passing on titles have a significant impact on a studios' cashflow and profit for these quarters.

The studio side of the negotiation process was more complex with many stakeholders seeking input to any new Redbox deal. *Studio's internal stakeholders* come from multiple levels of business affairs, operations, finance, and sales executives. These studio executives often have their year-end bonuses or other performance incentives tied to the agreement. There were also studio's *external stakeholders* such as movie investors, production partners, and profit participants whom the studio needed to satisfy. They wanted their studio to be in a Redbox deal when their DVD movie was released.

Lessons Learned From Redbox Negotiations

- Expect a highly competitive negotiation when the other side's business is declining and their management is unstable.
- Every negotiating side has leverage points; look to their market share and profit mix.
- Motivate internal stakeholders to gain their support in a difficult negotiation.
- Establishing an *us against them* mindset is effective getting stakeholder approval and cooperation entering a difficult negotiation.
- Public companies often take short-term quarterly gains over long-term vision.

CHAPTER 17

Movie Studio Negotiations

Part One: Redbox Versus Warner Bros., Fox, and Universal

Redbox Versus Warner Bros: Nothing Personal, Just Business

The Redbox–WBHE three-year deal was set to expire at the end of 2014. Redbox paid WBHE just under $100 million annually under the current deal. Before leaving WBHE, I had led the studio's negotiations against Redbox, but now it was my responsibility to lead the Redbox negotiations against WBHE.

I was hired by the Redbox president to negotiate the six expiring studios deals. He was an ex-WB president, a long-time colleague, and personal friend. Having his support in these difficult negotiations was critical for our successful negotiations. We knew the WBHE financials and operations better than anyone on the new WBHE negotiating team. Negotiating against your former company is like being able to see the competing hand in a poker game. A good tactic to gain a negotiation edge is hiring someone from the other side. It will pay for itself many times over.

The Redbox Edge

The first Redbox leverage point was the current deal expiring at the end of Warner Bros.'s 2014 fiscal year. We knew the WBHE 2015 financial plan was based on having a full-year of Redbox revenue. Not having a deal to start its financial year would put WBHE below-plan in the first quarter

2015. This situation created deadline pressure for WBHE. The side with the firmer deadline is vulnerable to be leveraged for better terms. Edge to Redbox.

The second Redbox leverage point was the revenue importance imbalance between the two parties. Redbox was the second largest revenue contributor to WBHE compared to WBHE being only the fifth highest rental generator for Redbox. The disparity created an imbalance of importance, which meant WBHE needed Redbox more than Redbox needed WBHE. Edge to Redbox.

The third Redbox leverage point was the weak Warner Bros. movie performance leading up to the contract expiration and projected into the first half of 2015. The WBHE performance becomes more important for the studio when it can mitigate box office underperformance. Being out of deal gives Redbox the option to pass on these weak WBHE titles and hurt WBHE performance financially. Edge to Redbox.

Our fourth leverage point was our ability to approach the negotiation as a *shrinking fixed sum* requiring a *competitive strategy*. This included the threat to go out of deal with a workaround plan. The WBHE approach was a *grow-the-pie* negotiation. They expected a *collaborative strategy* as the Redbox president and I recently left the studio. They were unaware of the intense financial pressures we faced to keep Redbox viable. We were going to negotiate hard. Edge to Redbox.

The fifth leverage point was knowing the new WBHE negotiators viewed the Redbox negotiations as an annoyance. They wanted to avoid "this shit show every three years." Knowing the other side wants to minimize their time negotiating means they are not confident in the outcome. The studio's attitude enabled us to set the tone and the pacing of the negotiation to our advantage. Edge to Redbox.

Our sixth leverage point was understanding the Warner Bros. studio management hierarchy and approval process. WBHE had assigned a mid-level sales VP to lead the negotiation. Due to the size of the deal, he did not have the authority to approve the terms. Once the other side knows you do not have the authority, it makes you less effective.

Finally, we knew the other studios would be observing how the Redbox–WBHE negotiation progressed. We wanted the other studios to know in advance that Redbox was going to negotiate hard for significant cost savings with every studio expiring deal. We thought the advanced notice would inform each studio's management that future revenue from any Redbox extension would be much less than previous years. What I learned was that studios are like spoiled children, each believing they are uniquely special and expect to get what they want.

WBHE Negotiator and WB Approver

Every layer of management approval adds difficulty and can impede the progress of a negotiation. The WBHE Domestic President and WB Global Distribution President, did not have approval authority on most of the terms of the deal. The final decision maker was the WB CEO Kevin Tsujihara who was three levels above the WBHE lead negotiator. Tsujihara held a weekly staff meeting with the WB division presidents on Mondays at 11:00 a.m. The tone of the meeting was collegial, but competitive. This is where Tsujihara would approve the Redbox deal terms. Our negotiation strategy was to work around the VP, frustrate the two presidents, and get to the ultimate decision maker *at the most opportunistic time.*

The Redbox and WBHE opening positions were $25 million apart in annual value. WBHE wanted to receive a $5 million annual increase in a three-year deal and Redbox countered with a $20 million annual cost savings in a two-year deal. Redbox wanted a shorter deal length to hedge against a declining DVD rental market. WB wanted a longer deal length to lock in stable above-market revenue.

WBHE positioned themselves as the home entertainment market leader and approached the negotiations from a superior position. They initially tried to control the negotiations by having the meetings on the studio lot, with their attorney physically papering the agreement. In this case, there was no advantage to WBHE as we would be removing all the WBHE favorable ambiguous language in the new agreement.

Redbox Strategy

Our plan was to use a *competitive strategy* with hard opening tactics to take away their assumptive superior position. Our starting position was Redbox would be out of deal at the end of the year and into the next fiscal quarter if WBHE did not agree to significant cost savings. We provided credible support for our position with movie-by-movie projections of the anticipated WBHE revenue shortfall being tens of million dollars.

The WBHE executives were shocked and disappointed this was not going to be an easy extension. They were upset at the competitive *take it or leave it* position, but we had a fiduciary responsibility to Redbox. This was not personal, just business. Feelings were hurt, and apparently, despite 20 years at the studio, we burned the bridge in one day.

We achieved our first negotiation objective of surpassing the VP. Future negotiation meetings would be tele-conferences with the WBHE president. The negotiation slowly progressed toward the end of WB fiscal year. To increase the frustration between the WBHE president and CEO, we started to give our counteroffers on Monday morning at 8:00. The WBHE president would not have time to develop a response by 11:00. We knew the CEO would ask if the Redbox deal was done, and the response would always be "I just got their counter, but I haven't had the time to evaluate it." CEOs want to make decisions and not wait for analyses. We knew this pressure would eventually give us the edge.

The studio internal frustration was growing as some of our old colleagues told us we were being major *pains in the ass* and increasing WBHE's desire to get this deal done. There is a fine line between being an effective negotiator and being a prick. We may have crossed the line.

The WBHE took the $5 million increase demand off the table but did not want to give cost savings near our $20 million target. The deal expired December 31, 2014. We started the new year by passing on the smaller movie titles released in the first quarter. On good-renting WBHE DVD titles, we bought a small quantity at Wal-Mart and gained additional revenue by selling them used. This disrupted WBHE inventory replenishment causing the studio to lose money. The WB cofinancers were made aware their movies would not be getting the Redbox revenue.

Redbox had an insurmountable negotiation edge. After six weeks, WBHE agreed to most of our cost-savings terms. Winning the first studio negotiation was important with the other studios lined up. On a personal basis, negotiating hard does have a downside. Despite being valued and appreciated Warner Bros. employees for 20 years, we were now *those Redbox pricks*.

Lessons Learned From Warner Bros. Negotiations

- Having support of management is critical when setting the negotiation strategy.
- The side with the firmer deadline is most vulnerable to time pressure and can expect to be leveraged as the deadline approaches.
- Hiring someone from the other negotiation team is a good investment for success.
- The side with the most vulnerability to market volatility will want a shorter deal to minimize risk.

Redbox Versus Fox: Know Your Role and Stay in Your Lane

By 2015, Fox Home Entertainment (FHE) had two years of excellent box office results and the leading market share along with distributing MGM/UA and DreamWorks Animation (DWA) movies. FHE continued to publicly express displeasure with the Redbox cannibalistic low-price business. The current four-week delay deal was expiring on June 30, 2015, at the end of the Fox fiscal year. Fox wanted to extend the expiring deal but was insisting on higher payments. Redbox rental activity was declining and needed lower payments to survive.

Negotiation Strategies

The FHE executives relished their company reputation as tough negotiators who go after every dollar on the table. They believed their strong box office performance and leading market share gave them the negotiation edge. They approached the negotiating with a *competitive strategy* wanting a bigger share of a zero-sum situation. Redbox countered with a *collaborative strategy*, sharing our declining rental data to support a lower cost deal.

Hollywood is a cyclical business, and a studio's past year performance means little for the coming year. We projected the 2015–2016 Fox movie slate to be much worse than prior years. Our negotiating objective was to pay below-market price for the lesser upcoming content. The studio fully expected to get an extension that was the best in the industry—the Sony deal terms but with a delay. Their attitude was "we are Fox, we lead home entertainment, we deserve it, so get it." We assumed the Fox CEO knew the Sony rental terms and expected his home entertainment president to get it.

Opening Positions

Like WBHE in the prior negotiation, FHE assumed the superior position with the first meeting being held on the studio lot. They filled the conference room with a dozen people from sales, marketing, operations, legal and finance departments, as well as their general manager and president. They all thought it was going to be an easy win. Everyone wanted to contribute to the victory of getting the best deal in the industry. The Redbox four attendees were the Redbox president, a buyer, an analytics person, and me. We opened the negotiations with a 20-minute presentation on the decline of the DVD rental market and a projected Fox 2015–2016 release schedule supporting why Redbox should pay Fox less money than the previous deal.

Fox politely listened, but as soon as the presentation was over, the barrage started. Each attendee took their turn piling on with rationale for a better deal. It was near the end of their fiscal year, so performance reviews and bonuses were top of mind. The Fox president gave the signal to cease fire and after a long pause said, "So, what do you think?" They genuinely believed we would agree to their higher opening offer in the first 30 minutes.

We needed to establish a crack in the negotiation foundation of their position. We focused on the two errors in their preparation. First, they overestimated their importance to Redbox. They thought their box office success directly translated to being the leading rental revenue generator for Redbox. Fox was ranked a distant fourth in revenue generation due to the poor renting DreamWorks animation movies, Fox Searchlight film acquisitions, and the MGM dramas. Second, FHE incorrectly assumed Redbox would be hurt by not being in deal. This was the optimal time for Redbox to go out of deal and implement the workaround operation.

Know Your Roles

Without showing confidential documents, we needed to convince FHE management all the other studios were getting less due to the declining rental market. FHE was starting to accept our data supporting the Fox underperformance of certain genres and box office levels movies. They knew their movie slate for the next two years was skewed to low-renting genres. We were close to getting agreement when our financial analyst, wanting to contribute in a positive way, let slip critical information that weakened our position. Fox caught it, questioned it, and quickly ended the meeting. All the hard work convincing them our data were correct ended in minutes. They rescheduled for the following week to review all the Redbox–Fox accounting statements to support their version of the truth.

There are two lessons to learn by this misstep. First, you must prepare better than the other side, especially if there is math involved. There can be no speculation or guessing on numbers, especially in accounting and finance areas of the agreement. Numbers must be transparent and vetted for accuracy. There is no margin of error. The best numbers win.

Second, everyone in the negotiation meeting room must know their role and stay within it. The ability to follow the negotiation communication strategy is dependent on cooperation among the attendees. Most staff members are well intentioned and want to make an impact. The leader must train them to stay within their roles. There should be a clear understanding who answers specific questions from the other side. No adding commentary or context to a direct answer. Make sure staff doesn't try to be the smartest person in the room. Conducting rehearsals is an effective way to make sure your team will perform to expectations.

Fox came back the following week with their aggressive opening position. The deadline was approaching, and we were prepared to go out of deal at the end of Fox's fiscal year. The projected Fox underperforming film slate over the next three months included the underperforming *Penguins of Madagascar* DreamWorks Animation title. It was time to escalate their internal pressure.

The Negotiation Dagger

A *negotiation dagger* is an action taken to leverage the other side's biggest vulnerability to gain an immediate win. It is best used late in the negotiations to close the deal. One of the biggest fears for a negotiator is when someone at a higher level is unhappy with your progress or results.

The Fox negotiation vulnerability was their distribution relationship with the DreamWorks Animation CEO, Jeffrey Katzenberg. He was a highly involved and demanding executive who expected and received a high level of attention in the DWA–Fox distribution agreement. If DWA did not think Fox maximized the revenue of a DWA asset, they would hold the Fox executives accountable. Going out of deal gave Redbox the opportunity to pass on the DWA *Penguins of Madagascar* DVD. This dagger would disappoint Katzenberg—something everyone at FHE wanted to avoid.

Through industry relationships, we let a senior DWA executive know we were not buying their title if there was no deal. The lost revenue to DWA would be of a couple of million dollars. The news quickly got back to the right people. The FHE negotiators expressed their displeasure for using a back channel to pressure them at the deadline.

Sometimes negotiations are less about the money and more about ego. FHE needed to be able to tell their studio management they got a better deal than the previous one. We needed to pay Fox less in a declining market. *Our negotiating objective needed to fit their negotiating goal.* Acknowledging both, we were able to construct a new flexible deal paying FHE more if their slate and the DVD rental market improved, and less if either factor did not. FHE executives could pride themselves on getting *better terms*, and Redbox got the required cost savings by having more buying flexibility in a declining market.

Lessons Learned From Fox Negotiations

- Superior analytics give you the negotiation edge.
- Know your numbers and when best to use them.
- Know your role and stay in it.
- Use back channels to leverage their stakeholders but only once and at the optimal time.

Redbox Versus Universal: What's in It for Me?

Universal box office performance was typically between $1.2 and $1.5 billion annually, making it the fourth largest studio. Their slate was comprised of big movie franchises, including *Jurassic Park* and *The Despicables*, along with mid-level budgeted comedy and action films. Their growth strategy was dependent on acquiring numerous independent films under their Focus Features independent banner and their distribution partner STX. Universal Home Entertainment (UHE) large quantity of small movies made them more dependent on the Redbox revenue, which gave us the negotiation edge.

The Redbox–UHE negotiation at the end of 2015 was the last of the three delayed studios. There is no upside when you are the third entity to negotiate a similar deal. UHE was not going to get a better deal than Warner or Fox. Word had spread through the industry of the Redbox *competitive negotiation strategy* of going out of deal to get lower costs. The previous Redbox–UHE deals had been quickly negotiated with a *collaborative strategy* as both parties were aligned. UHE expected the same strategy but did not want to accept lower terms consistent with the DVD rental decline.

Management Disruptions

What should have been a smooth negotiation was made more complex and difficult by two recent organizational events at Redbox and Universal. First, new Outerwall CEO forced the Redbox president, my negotiating partner, to leave the company. I was to continue to lead the negotiations, but the CEO and CFO wanted to be more involved. I no longer had the trust and support of Redbox management. The previous UHE content deal had been negotiated by the Redbox CFO and general counsel. Both were not happy being relegated to support roles when I was hired. Going forward, the new process would be a negotiation by committee. Adding more *cooks* can provide more critical thinking and new ideas, but it requires more time for increased communication, analytics, teamwork, and trust. The new CEO emphasized the critical need to get significant cost reductions and improved cash flow. I heard the same mantra when Nabisco was put in play for a sale. It was no surprise when I later learned he was hired to sell the company. The clock was ticking!

On the other side of the table, Universal was going through management changes as well. I had begun negotiating with the long-time UHE senior VP of sales, but he was leaving the company. There would be a new president of UHE arriving from the UK who would lead the negotiations. His supervisor, the president of Universal Distribution, had final approval on the new deal. This president had responsibility for all content distribution deals across theaters, broadcast networks, retailers, streaming platforms, and specialty outlets such as kiosks. Obviously, you earn this position by having very strong negotiation skills, but the last thing he wanted to do was to take a meeting with a vending machine company. I still believed Redbox had the advantage as they needed our cash and knew nothing about our business.

Personal Incentives and Deadlines

The Redbox–UHE deal was expiring December 31, 2015, the end of their fiscal year. The expiring Redbox–Universal deal was worth just under $90 million annually under normal conditions, but the market was declining, and we wanted to pay 25 percent less. We projected the 2015–2016 UHE release schedule would be underperforming. This would require UHE to acquire a much higher number of independent films to mitigate their financial shortfall. By going out of deal, Redbox could create leverage with the threat of passing on these acquired smaller films. Edge to Redbox.

The UHE executives pressed unusually hard to have a signed Redbox deal by the end of their fiscal year. It was evident the deadline meant more to them than it did to us. We learned why in an unusual way. Redbox had an opening for an entry-level analyst position, and we interviewed a UHE financial analyst. During the initial interview process, he let us know the importance of the Redbox deal in UHE's annual performance targets. Edge to Redbox.

UHE DVD release schedule was loaded with small underperforming movies in the first quarter 2016. We used our analytics to show the new Redbox CEO the financial benefits of going out of deal with Universal for first three months of 2016. It is common industry practice for theaters and retailers to negotiate hard for favorable deal terms when a studio is having a run of poor movie performances. Conversely, studios negotiate hard to get favorable terms when their box office is exceeding expectations.

Our opening offer gave them select favorable terms on the big movies, but capped the number of smaller films Redbox would be required to take. The middle of their slate was the sticking point. Their mid-sized movies had an equal number of good renting genres (action, horror, and comedy) and bad renting genres (dramas, foreign, and period pieces). We discussed a deal structure that would provide equitable buying formula dependent on the genres. While appearing fair to both sides, it would generate lower costs for Redbox. Edge to Redbox.

The Impasse

We were close but now at an impasse as Universal was adamant about not accepting less money. A good negotiation tactic when an agreement is close, but at an impasse, is to meet in a fun social gathering. The event needs to be special so that the other side will be enthusiastic. The purpose is to foster honest, straightforward dialogue. We invited the Universal negotiating team to Seattle for a Saturday night dinner, a Sunday brunch, and a Seattle Seahawk football game in the Redbox luxury suite. The plan was to agree on final terms Saturday night, enjoy the activities on Sunday, and upon returning to Los Angeles on Monday morning, sign the deal. They agreed to come, but the Universal Distribution president would fly up for the Sunday brunch expecting to approve the last few deal terms.

The Saturday night dinner went well as the two negotiating teams enjoyed each other socially. Down to the final two deal items, we were poised to compromise to complete the deal in the morning. When we met for the Sunday brunch at the hotel, the tone of the gathering had changed. The UHE negotiating team said they were not going to budge on the last two items, and they want to rework some previously agreed to terms. The downside of socializing over a deal is not having a written record of what was agreed to. We spent most of the brunch recalling "you said," then "I said."

A negotiation grenade exploded when we asked when the Universal Distribution president would be arriving. They said, "He is in the limousine outside and won't come in or go to the game unless you agree to these terms, now." They added, "If he doesn't come in, we all fly back to LA now." This was very odd behavior, even for a movie studio. They are using the threat of *not* attending an NFL game in a luxury suite to get better deal terms. Imagine if we invited them up and did not allow them to attend the game unless they agreed to our terms?

Their president was using a tactic I call "throwing lightning bolts from above." He believed his superior position in the industry provided a negotiation edge. What he did not realize was the Redbox revenue to UHE was more important than UHE revenue to Redbox. Universal would be hurt if we went out of deal and did a workaround. Money always wins over status. Intimidating behavior is rarely productive and usually hardens the other side's resolve.

There is a point of *unproductivity* when both negotiating teams cannot close the deal because one or both deal-approvers sit hard on their positions. When a deal is close and both sides are dug in, it is best to have the two decision makers speak directly to each other to finalize the deal. We suggested the Universal Distribution president go to the game where he could discuss the remaining issues with the Redbox CEO in the luxury suite. During the game, the Universal Distribution president and Outerwall CEO were cordial and expressed desire to get an agreement, although neither one compromised their position on the remaining terms.

UHE increased the pressure through the December holidays after more unproductive sessions. The Redbox negotiation-by-committee was divided on how to get to an agreement. My position was to go out of deal to realize the cost savings as that tactic worked with Warner and Fox. Others wanted to compromise on the remaining items to maintain the studio relationship. The rationale was being in deal demonstrates industry support for wanting Redbox to survive. Another point is that, being in a deal keeps our retail merchandising costs on budget.

Deadline Compromise

As the year-end expiration deadline approached, there was an increased sense of desperation from the Universal side. The Universal Distribution president called us to his office on the final day and demanded a deal on the spot. He was less concerned about the specific deal terms as he was with just getting a signed agreement that day. We were joined by the Redbox CFO who wanted an agreement as well. We had to agree to ordering titles whose order dates had past, to avoid Universal taking a loss on those films in the first quarter. Redbox was able to get the other concessions necessary to generate the target cost savings for a multiyear deal.

Lessons Learned From Universal Negotiations

- When at a final impasse, have the highest authority from each side meet privately. Each should be prepared to reach an agreement.
- Closing deals at the deadline may require a shift to a compromise strategy.
- When neither side's lead negotiator can approve the deal, the negotiation will take longer.
- Knowing the incentives of the other side's key stakeholders is an advantage.

CHAPTER 18

Movie Studio Negotiations

Part Two: Redbox Versus Disney, Lionsgate, Paramount, and Sony

Redbox Versus Disney: You're in the Penalty Box

Disney was the only studio with the *high-risk, high-reward* movie slate consisting of only a dozen big-budget movies. These costly franchise films generate huge revenues from theaters, licensed merchandise, and DVD retail sales, but the DVD rental revenue was relatively small. Disney and Redbox were in a unique situation where neither partner needed a direct relationship to be successful. Disney believed their high-quality franchise films had the highest rate of Redbox cannibalization than the other studios. They were the only studio not compelled to agree to a three-year $300 million contract with Redbox.

A few years before, Disney was close to making a very favorable multiyear deal with Redbox. Disney insisted on the best terms in the industry as the market leader and being the last studio to negotiate a deal. Redbox management believed having Disney in a deal would have little impact on the financial performance, but analysts favored stable content flow and relationships when evaluating Redbox.

Negotiations started and stopped numerous times over the years. Then Disney introduced a $25 retail-priced multidisc package strategy, enabling consumers to view a Disney movie three ways: a Blu Ray disc, a DVD disc, and a downloadable digital code of the movie. Redbox realized the new Disney combo packs were much more profitable than having a deal. The combo packs would give Redbox four revenue streams: rent the Blu Ray disc, rent DVD disc, sell the digital codes to an online distributors, and sell previously viewed Disney Blu Rays and DVDs to distress wholesalers.

Redbox ended the negotiations, which angered the Disney lead negotiator. Executives never forget being embarrassed by another company. They carry it with them and seek revenge later.

By 2016, the previous Redbox CEO, who ended the negotiation with Disney, was no longer at Redbox. Believing this was a personal issue between the lead negotiators, we reached out to the Disney Distribution President to determine if she would be interested in discussing a new deal. The amount of lost revenue was not large enough to offset the disappointment. The response we received was, "I have no interest in Redbox. I don't care about your numbers. Redbox is in the penalty box until I say you're not."

Lessons Learned From Disney Negotiations

- Launching a new product into the market during a negotiation is very risky.
- Keep management informed of the negotiation status, but never signal a deal is done until it is physically signed.
- Avoid embarrassing the other side's lead negotiator as it will cause problems later.
- Sometimes the best deal is no deal.

Redbox Versus Lionsgate: Something Is Leaking

Lionsgate is a mini-major studio with a relatively low annual domestic box office of about $600 million. They had some successful franchise movies: *HUNGER GAMES*, *JOHN WICK*, and *SAW*. However, their slate was mostly built by acquiring low-budget action and horror films. Those genres rent very well on DVD. They were the third studio to sign a below-market day and date deal with Redbox. At that time, the negotiations were collaborative as both parties understood the mutually beneficial relationship. Lionsgate believed Redbox rentals were highly incremental revenue, and Redbox needed low-cost content with rental-friendly action and horror genres.

The Lionsgate executives forged a strong relationship with the Redbox executives over the years. As guests of Lionsgate, Redbox executives attended Hollywood premieres, award shows, and other Los Angeles-based entertainment industry outings. In return, Lionsgate executives traveled to Seattle to attend NFL games in the Redbox luxury suite at Seattle Seahawk's Lumen stadium. The executives on both sides genuinely liked and respected each other.

Opposing Opening Positions

The 2014 Lionsgate contract renewal was my first negotiation for Redbox. They were the smallest studio in the market and needed Redbox to achieve their financial goals. The current contract was the most favorable Redbox agreement of all the studio deals, yet I was determined to validate my hiring and improve upon it. The deal term I wanted to lower was the high number of nontheatrical films Redbox was required to buy. This category of film sometimes included poor renting direct-to-video family and teen genres. I proposed a significant reduction in our requirement to buy this type of film. Having just arrived from Warner Bros., I thought Lionsgate was vulnerable. Unfortunately, there was one aspect I had overlooked in the negotiation.

Lionsgate knew they had a below-market deal and wanted a better one. They proposed a small increase in the minimum guarantee and to raise the number of low-budget, direct-to-video films Redbox was required to buy. I countered to the Lionsgate EVP with holding the minimum guarantee at current levels and reducing the cap number to give Redbox flexibility for movies outside of the deal. This posed a significant risk to the overall Lionsgate business model of aggressively buying independent films based on the expected Redbox revenue. Talks had stalled, and the current deal was about to expire putting Lionsgate revenue at risk. I had recommended to the Redbox president and Outerwall CEO that we go out of deal, let them feel the pain of a few missed titles, and then reopen the negotiation. I wanted to use a *competitive negotiation strategy* as we had the negotiation edge. What I overlooked was the relationship factor.

The Importance of Relationships

The Lionsgate Home Entertainment CEO called the Seattle-based Outerwall CEO and CFO to complain about being squeezed excessively hard on the new deal. When I discussed my progress to our C-suite, they suggested to extend the current deal with only minor changes. I was told not to disrupt the Redbox business by going out of deal. When I presented the modified terms to the Lionsgate negotiator, he immediately agreed to all of them. It was then I realized there was a *back channel collaborative negotiation* without me knowing it. Someone on my team was giving my progress to the CEO. I was naïve to think, as a new employee, I would be allowed to negotiate autonomously. I should have known the past relationships had a weighted value in negotiations. Edge to Lionsgate.

Managing Leaks

Prior to the negotiation, I should have determined who in our organization had the key relationships with the other side. When there is a prior relationship, you should know who they are and how to use it to your advantage. Business relationships are highly valued and are based on a mutually beneficial exchange of information. These previous relationships take precedent in a new negotiation. You cannot prevent the communication from happening. The best a negotiation leader can do is keep the confidential information inside a tight, trusted circle.

Your in-house attorney is one to rely on for the truth about leaks. They understand the importance of confidentiality. Solicit their help to reduce the exposure. Their litigation abilities can help structure questions to the staff to identify and manage leaks. Also, planned leaks can be used to your advantage by planting false information to the leakers. Publicity executives have the internal and external sources to exploit relationships with misinformation to your advantage.

Lessons Learned From Lionsgate Negotiations

- Negotiation leaders should be the only person permitted to discuss any aspects of the deal with the other side, but this is hard to achieve.
- The negotiating team members having previous relationships with the other side make confidentiality leaks possible and difficult to suppress.
- Disbursing misinformation can be effective when there are confidentiality leaks.
- Attorneys and publicity executives respect confidentiality and know how to leverage misinformation.

Redbox Versus Paramount: Please, Not Now

In early 2016, the Paramount movie studio was going through difficult times with a boardroom battle, management restructuring, poor cash flow, and underperforming box office. The studio desperately needed cash to finance their movie productions and was actively soliciting investors. Paramount Home Entertainment (PHE) top management had recently changed with a newly promoted president and SVP of sales. PHE's lucrative seven-year deal with Redbox was set to expire in September 2016. Redbox payments for content accounted for nearly half of PHE annual revenue. However, the decline in the DVD rental market made the output deal so one-sided, Redbox was losing money on most of the Paramount releases by the start of 2016. Edge to Paramount.

No Relief in Sight

Paramount was not going to give Redbox any relief before the deal ended. They were happy to let this deal run its course until the end of September. In this situation, they did not value the relationship, only the guaranteed revenue for every movie they released. Knowing the mentality of movie studios, I understood their actions. You would be fired for proposing to accept less money from an overly favorable contract when your studio is having financial difficulties.

Outside Financial Implications

I was eager to begin the negotiations early in 2016 because the new deal was going to generate hundreds of millions in cost savings for Redbox. The PHE president and SVP of sales each knew whoever was going to negotiate the deal would eventually be scapegoated and fired. During a casual conversation at an industry event, the PHE SVP of sales said he wanted to set up the first meeting to discuss the new deal. He did not give a timeframe despite the deal expiring in six months. It was months before he arranged a meeting.

I understood why he personally did not want to begin negotiating, but there was another factor causing the avoidance. Paramount was actively soliciting outside investors, which created a legal obligation to inform them of any material change in their ongoing business. Paramount did not want to inform potential investors of an expected hundreds of million revenue reduction in a new Redbox deal. Their solution to avoid any improprieties was to ignore the upcoming contract expiration date. Paramount did not want any new deal meetings, proposals, or discussions until their management turmoil was settled, and they secured their new funding.

Redbox for Sale

Complicating the Paramount–Redbox negotiation process further, the publicly held Outerwall was now soliciting offers to be sold. The main attraction of Redbox was the improved operating profit coming from the significantly reduced content cost in the new deals. Paramount and Redbox were both comfortable, for the same legal and fiduciary reasons, letting the deal expire in September 2016. In 2017, Outerwall was purchased by Apollo Capital and a new Redbox–PHE deal with the significantly lower terms was signed.

Lesson Learned From Paramount Non-Negotiations

- Avoid being the lead negotiator when there are unrealistic expectations from management.
- Knowing the motivations of the other side will enable you to understand their behavior.
- When there are personal career incentives to not do a deal, it will not get done.

Redbox Versus Sony: Be a Good Partner.
No, You Be a Good Partner

In 2009, Sony Pictures Home Entertainment (SPHE) was the first studio to break ranks with the industry and sign a seven-year, day and date Redbox output deal worth twice market rate. The deal required Redbox to buy *every film Sony distributed* at a prearranged price and quantities regardless of rental potential. The Sony Pictures slate had a few family animated hits such as *CLOUDY WITH A CHANCE OF MEATBALLS*, *TRANSYLVANIA*, and *SMURFS*. However, they took advantage of their Redbox and international TV distribution output deals to acquire an industry-high number of independent films. Edge to SPHE.

By the end of 2015, most of the independent movie production and art house theaters went out of business due to competition from digital streamers. Sony took advantage of this oversupply of unreleased indie films by acquiring them and putting them through their output deals. Most of these movies were unprofitable for Redbox. Thankfully, the deal was set to expire at the end of September 2016. Coincidentally, the Apollo acquisition of Outerwall/Redbox was going to close in September as well.

Redbox was looking forward to a new deal to stem the SPHE losses. We were confident in our ability to get hundreds of millions in cost savings having successfully negotiated new lower-cost contracts with Warner Bros., Fox, Universal, and Lionsgate. There was no pressure from Apollo to have an SPHE deal extension as they knew Redbox would benefit financially being out of deal. Edge to Redbox.

SPHE Bad Assumptions

The SPHE president, who made the original deal, had been replaced by a Sony international TV distribution executive. The new president made numerous flawed assumptions heading into the Redbox negotiations in 2016. First, he was overconfident thinking the little vending machine company desperately needed a direct deal with SPHE to survive. He did not understand the effectiveness of our workaround operation. Second, he believed the imminent Apollo–Outerwall sale gave SPHE a deadline advantage that would force Redbox to compromise and extend the current deal. The exact opposite was true. Third, he thought the negotiation tone would be friendly and collaborative because SPHE gave Redbox their first studio deal. He underestimated the Redbox resolve to engage in a tough *competitive negotiation* despite hearing it from all the other studios. Lastly, he assumed nobody from the Redbox negotiating team would be around after the Apollo deal was completed. Why even bother with these people when there would be new negotiators next month. He was mostly right with this one, but edge to Redbox.

The Impasse

By August 2016, my negotiations with the Sony business development and business affairs executives had reached an impasse. They realized there was not going to be a deal extension with the same terms. We remained firm about getting cost savings aligned with the long-term DVD industry decline. The SPHE president knew he could not offset the hundreds of millions in lost revenue in the new deal, and it was going to cost him his job. He tried one last desperate effort to get a favorable Redbox deal.

With two months before the current deal expired, SPHE went nuclear trying to get Redbox to *compromise.* Per the current deal terms, SPHE forced Redbox to buy 60 unprofitable films in the final two months of the deal generating significant losses for Redbox. The SPHE president thought that by severely hurting Redbox profitability right before the sale, Apollo would reconsider the acquisition. SPHE offered to stop the forced buying if Redbox would agree to extend the current deal on a month-to-month basis until a final agreement could be reached. The strategy did not work as Apollo knew the large financial advantage of being out of deal with SPHE by October.

When in a stalemate, it is a best practice to have the two leaders of the organizations meet. In this case, I was not confident in any resolutions. The Outerwall CEO and SPHE president were new to their positions, neither understood nor cared about the other's business. Still, if progress was to be made, these two needed to go head-to-head. I believe each leader wanted to meet the other guy who was trying to hurt them. As it was the last studio negotiation, I thought it would be fun to watch.

The Showdown

Like every studio before them, Sony took the superior position by having us meet on the studio lot. The president thought the new Outerwall CEO would be in awe of the surroundings. Studio executives have a strong feeling of pride working at a place everyone loves. My previous Warner Bros. office looked over the studio lot. It was directly above the WB studio tours, where hundreds of people paid $50 to visit my workplace daily. It was understandable how the new SPHE president believed there was an advantage over a Chicago-based vending machine company. They could not have been more wrong. The only reason the Outerwall CEO was going to the meeting on the Sony lot was to meet the person who was punishing their largest revenue provider.

The room was filled with many SPHE executives, while Redbox attendees were the CEO, CFO, a video buyer, and me. The SPHE president started the meeting saying how great this relationship has been the last seven years, even though he only arrived two years prior. He failed to read the room as he continued to pontificate on how great the current deal is and we would be smart to extend it. Each time he referred to the deal as being *great*, it just made our CEO angrier. Finally, the Outerwall CEO had heard enough. "If you are such a good partner, why are you forcing us to take all these unprofitable movies? What kind of partner exploits a loophole, forcing your biggest vendor to lose money?"

Their president responded with great hubris in a condescending manner, "SPHE is the market leader, who made Redbox the success it is today. SPHE deserves an extension of the current deal but we will throw you a bone and take a little less money – but only a little less. You should be happy to have such a great partner as us."

The Outerwall CEO stood up and leaned forward saying there is no way we were going to extend the deal and continue to lose money. He explained how once the deal expired Redbox would use the workaround operation causing SPHE to receive about 10 percent of the revenue it is enjoying now. The SPHE president realized this little vending machine company was going to cause an insurmountable problem.

The SPHE president stood up, leaned over the table, pointed his finger and said, "You need to be a good partner and extend the deal." The Outerwall CEO, still standing, leaned closer and pointed his finger saying,

"You need to be a good partner and stop losing us money." Like petulant children, both sat down and just stared at each other for a few minutes. The SPHE president smugly asked the Outerwall CEO how the Apollo acquisition was coming. The CEO turned over the last negotiation card saying the deal is expected to close very soon with the expectations of not being in deal with Sony for a long time. Having realized the last piece of leverage was off the table, The SPHE president now understood he lost the negotiation. The rest of us in the room exchanged knowing grins understanding how hard it is negotiating an agreement when leadership has unrealistic expectations.

The Final Word

The SPHE president suggested a follow-up meeting after the Apollo deal closes knowing there would be a new CEO. His only strategy was to play the waiting game. The delay allowed for more time for him to find other areas of revenue. The SPHE president knew when he eventually informed his management of the decrease in Redbox revenue, he would be exiting the company. The Outerwall CEO knew he would be leaving the company after the deal closed. The two leaders shook hands knowing they would never see each other again.

In September 2016, Apollo Capital purchased Outerwall/Redbox stock for $1.6 billion. Redbox would go out of deal with Sony for a long time saving *hundreds of million dollars* in content costs. The Outerwall CEO and I left the company after the completion of the Apollo deal. The SPHE president left the company in early 2018.

Lessons Learned From the Sony Negotiation

- There is a high probability of getting the best deal terms being the first of your competitors to sign a long-term deal in a volatile market.
- Monitor the deals to ensure they still work for both partners. If not, adjust accordingly to maintain a productive longer-term relationship.
- Confirm you understand the other side's business levers so that your assumptions are accurate.
- Know how to be a good partner.

Epilogue

Negotiate Coming and Going

Get Paid to Leave Your Job

On a Tuesday morning, in September 2016, I drove to the Redbox office in suburban Los Angeles feeling nervous, a little uncertain, and a sense of dread. But as I entered the parking lot, my feelings changed to calm, somewhat relieved, and sense of closure. The end to a challenging year was here. As the Senior Vice-President of Content and Marketing at Redbox, I had known for months this day would be an experience like no other in my 30-year career. Walking from the parking lot to the Redbox office, I felt like a leprechaun about to get the pot of gold at the end of the rainbow. But I knew when private equity closes a deal, older leprechauns tend to disappear.

The previous business day, Apollo Capital Management, a private equity firm, announced the completion of their purchase of Outerwall, Inc., the holding company for Redbox, Coinstar, and EcoATM, for $1.6 billion. Financially, this was a good thing as Apollo bought all the stock I had accumulated as a senior executive. However, when a private equity firm buys a company, their first action is to aggressively cut costs. My age and compensation made me low-hanging fruit on the Redbox cost-savings tree.

I was the first one in the office. I arrived at my desk, put down my bag, and turned on my company-owned desktop computer. My password was not allowing me into my company files. You know it's going to be a tough day when your password doesn't work. After several failed attempts, I looked up to see the Outerwall HR representative standing at my office door. We recognized each other from working together for the past year on several companywide layoffs. Ironically, I used to be the angel of death standing in the doorway and asking the startled employee if they *had a minute.* The HR rep gave the cliched apology that it wasn't personal, just doing his job. Of course it's not personal to use a company-approved statement to say, "Hello" to a colleague.

He expressed appreciation I knew the company's exit process. I handed over my company credit card and ID badge. I removed my personal laptop from my bag and opened my email account. Within minutes, he scanned my personal files wiping out any communication having the words, *Outerwall, Redbox, negotiation,* or *contracts.* He inspected my bag for company documents, finding none. He handed me a packet of papers detailing my separation agreement, which I had negotiated at my hiring. I knew my stock options were vested, my severance payment and health care options were set. I signed the agreement; we shook hands, and I walked out of the office. The six-minute termination was a quick ending to my Redbox employment—just the way the company and I wanted it. I learned this valuable lesson with my previous employment at Warner Bros.—negotiate your exit at the end the hiring process. Companies appreciate the discussion because they don't want any loose ends, such as incomplete business deals or postemployment lawsuits.

Lessons Learned From Redbox

- Exit wounds heal faster when you are paid to leave your job.
- Every employment comes to an end. Negotiate your exit plan *well before* it happens.
- The key to negotiating your exit during the hiring process is timing and tone.
- How you leave a company is as important as how you arrive.

Glossary

Agenda: List of meeting items to be discussed and goals to be achieved in priority order. The creator and owner of the agenda control the meeting.

Agent: Person who represents an entity in the negotiation with partial or full responsibility. Best to know other side's personal and professional motivation as well as compensation.

Anchoring the Discussion: Establishing one side or level of the discussion from which all subsequent conversations will be based. Usually established with the first credible offer.

Arbitration: Process to resolve a no-progress negotiation where a *third party* evaluates both sides, renders a judgment, and implements a binding solution.

Aspiration Base: A realistic view of the highest possible outcome of a negotiated agreement. Be careful as this may become the standard for your evaluation and reputation.

Auction: Bidding process designed to increase competition when there are multiple interested parties. The competitive nature will irrationally drive up the price.

Bargaining Zone: The negotiation space between the initial offer and the counteroffer or the *walk-away* positions of the two parties. The space will evolve as the negotiation continues.

Bargaining: Fluid competitive position in a *zero-sum* or *distributive* negotiation process that claims value rather than creating value.

Barter Trade Agreement: When one party exchanges a good or service to an entity or multiple entities, who in return, delivers other goods or services to the originating party. Commonly used in international trade when local currencies are too unstable.

BATNA: Best alternative to a negotiated agreement is a preferred course of action in the absence of a deal. Popularized by Bazerman as well as Fischer and Ury.

Bear Hug: An acquisition strategy when the buyer is willing to pay an above-market price to ensure the owners will sell.

Brinkmanship: The tactic of trying to achieve an advantageous outcome by pushing to the rational limit of the other side. The hard ball tactic is utilized when the others side has no viable alternative.

Bogey Tactic: Early in the process pretending a low-value item is really important to you, and later, it is traded for something of greater value.

Claw Back: When one party tries to change a previously approved term to their favor.

Coalition: When two parties temporarily join forces deriving mutual benefits and a competitive advantage in a multiparty negotiation.

Collective Bargaining: Process by which large parties negotiate in *everyone's best interest*, especially when one side holds a significant advantage. Commonly used in employment and union contracts.

Common Ground: Terms of agreement between parties. Best to identify early in the negotiation process to determine the quantity and quality of effort required to complete the negotiation.

Compliance Transparency: Deal point requiring exposure to what was agreed to throughout the length of the deal, specifically service levels and quality of goods.

Concession Strategy: Prenegotiation plan to identify what terms one side is willing to give in order to get something of equal or greater value in return. These are not *needs* but *wants* in your priority list. Also called the trading plan.

Constituent: Person or party, such as company peer or union to whom the negotiator is held accountable and therefore has internal influence on the outcome. Also called stakeholders.

Contingency Clause: A clause in the contract to provide additional benefits or an *out* by one party if the value of the completed deal becomes highly unfavorable to that party. The clause provides incremental benefits to the party once thresholds are met or exceeded.

Crunch Response: Instructions to change specific items in the offer. Utilized instead of a counteroffer when the original offer is unrealistic or contains misinformation.

Dance of the First Offer: When two parties go *back and forth* determining who will make the first offer.

Day and Date: An entertainment industry term for timing of new content release. The *day* is the day of the week, and the *date* is self-explanatory. Movies are released on Fridays, while packaged media, (movies/games/music) and transactional video on demand (TVOD) are usually released on Tuesdays.

Distributive Negotiation: Utilized in a *Fixed Sum* or *Win–Lose* situation mainly with a single or few terms, where one side measurably will gain more than the other side either by paying higher or lower than market level price for a good or service.

End Run: When one party attempts to make progress by avoiding the other side's negotiation team and contacting their decision maker or person of influence to improve their position. Best utilized with a confidential third party making the contact to avoid being called out for untrustworthy behavior. Usually occurs when a long impasse has occurred.

Exploding Offer: Offer that will no longer be considered after a firm deadline.

Facilitator: Single person or entity mutually hired by multiple parties in a complex negotiation to aid in the process of completing an agreement. Best used in a completely new situation and the parties have little mutual knowledge. The facilitator has no authority or the capability to direct a binding conclusion.

Framing: Identifying the boundaries of the negotiation. Implemented after the initial counteroffer and adjusted as the process unfolds. Creates common understanding of the outstanding issues and identifies progress necessary to close the gap between the parties.

Fortifying Tactics: Competitive negotiation tactic deployed prematurely to establish a position and reduce the need for concessions.

Game Theory: Mathematical modeling in mostly *zero sum* and *non-cooperative* interactive behavior between rational parties. There is no morality or ethics involved—simply math. Game examples are Prisoners Dilemma, Stag Hunt, Chicken and Dictator.

Gazumping: When the buyer accepts a bid from one party, then later accepts another high bid from another party.

Joint Venture: A multiple-party agreement combining select resources in pursuit of a common goal, which is usually a prorated share of revenue, costs, and profits.

Integrative Negotiation: Referred to as the *Win–Win* or *Grow the Pie* process. Best utilized when there are multiple issues/terms with high complexity and long-term partnerships are involved. Emphasizes collaboration and places a high value on the relationship between parties.

Irrational Escalation: Wanting to win at any cost, continuing on a course of action beyond rational thought. The escalator usually wins and ends up with the winners curse.

Interest-Based Negotiation: A strategy in which both sides begin by stating their interests, so common ground is established, instead of one side offering a proposal. Best used in integrative or win–win negotiations.

Information Asymmetry: When one party has more information than the other.

Key Components Document: An internal management document consisting of deadline, leader, stakeholders, other side's interest, and market conditions details. Used as the discussion document with management, staff, and stakeholders to recommend proceeding with a negotiation.

Letter of Intent (LOI): The formal document containing the key terms of a proposed new deal that begins the negotiation process. Also known as memo of understanding (MOU).

Log Rolling: The process of making concessions by trading one asset, service, or specific issue for another of perceived equal value. Best to scorecard both parties log rolling activity to ensure the aggregate is equal or to your advantage. Also known as trade-offs.

Lose–Lose: When a negotiation fails to provide benefits to both parties usually due to personality conflicts or missed deadline. Uncontrollable outside factors can be marketplace variability forcing a suboptimal result.

Lose–Win: A distributive negotiation when one party is competing for fixed resource with the other side. Also known as a *fixed pie* where price is the main issue. Also known as win–lose.

Majority Rule: An agreed to decision-making process invoked during a multiparty negotiation to resolve issues. Best to have unanimous agreement to a formalized voting process. Informal *voting* can provide direction but is susceptible to domination by a vocal minority.

Mediation: Third-party catalyst helps conflicting parties with the negotiation process focusing on communication and rationale thought.

Memorandum of Understanding: A formal, nonbinding document stating the initial positions and willingness to start a negotiation toward an imminent binding agreement.

Moving the Goal Posts: Communicating the value of your needs to get the deal completed. When the other side agrees to the value, you increase the value of the needs or create additional needs.

Multiple Offer Strategy: Utilized in an integrative negotiation as a response to an early unrealistic anchoring by the other side. The alternative offers of equal value will reveal what issues are more important to the other side. Strategy is also used near the deadline to cause extra work or confusion in an effort to extending the deadline. Also known as multiple economic equivalent proposals (MEEP).

Negotiation Dagger: The exploitation of a major weak point in the other side's position that ends the negotiation your favor. Best used toward the end of the negotiation to bring an abrupt close of the deal.

Negotiators Dilemma: When neither party has enough information to move the discussions forward.

Nibble: The other side's small request at the end of a negotiation having low, current economic value. This may have greater economic value in future years. Nibble back at 2X the value, but in a different area of the agreement to curtail additional nibbling behavior.

Offensive Tactics: Actions taken in a competitive negotiation to stimulate concessions and accommodations from the other side.

Output Deal: Entertainment industry term when a distributor must buy and exploit all the content a studio, network, or production entity produces or acquires.

Paper the Deal: The physical writing of the agreement.

Partisan Perception: A biased favorable view of the negotiation from one side. Need to see the deal from their side—objectively. Can be minimized or avoided by using an objective third-party.

Pillars of the Agreement: The main terms of a negotiation proposal listed in the letter of intent or memorandum of understanding: product or service, length of agreement, geography, and payment terms.

Position-Based Negotiation: The traditional process of both parties stating their respective positions at the beginning of a negotiation and then work toward finding a mutually acceptable solution.

Principled Negotiation: Addresses issues of conflict between parties. Often used in an integrative approach to improve the situation as a whole with each party addressing their own issue-related behavior to create a mutually beneficial outcome. Also known as conflict management or conflict resolution.

Prisoner's Dilemma: A game theory example where two rational participants may not cooperate, although it will lead to an optimal outcome for both. The participants' self-interest and lack of trust impacts the outcome.

Prospect Theory: Evaluate risk depending on the current situation where some are more sensitive to loss than appreciative of gain. If the other side is risk-adverse, will accept lower value, but need higher certainty so the negotiation will be a difficult process of an aggregation of concessions/protections/loss avoidance. The opposite behavior is *Lottery*. Developed by Kahneman and Tversky.

Reciprocation: An exchange of items of like value such as information or concessions to reflect cooperation and trust. It is especially important in a integrative negotiation to demonstrate you are seeking a mutual benefit. Also known as gives and gets.

Red Herring: Introducing a new tangential or unrelated issue to divert the attention of the other side's top priorities in order to gain a strategic or tactical advantage.

Reservation Price: Least favorable price a party is willing to accept to complete the deal. Also known as the walk-away price. Also known as least acceptable agreement (LAA).

Schmuck Insurance: Additional clause to provide one party with additional benefits or an *out* if something highly unexpected occurs that radically favors or disadvantages one of the parties after the deal is completed. Also known as contingency clause.

Secure Agreement: Hedged or limited agreement due to lack of trust between parties.

Sequential Yes Factor: Getting each side to say *yes* to a string of terms creates a positive psychological effect on the negotiation.

Spoilers: One of the parties in a multiparty deal that has no incentive to agreeing to a deal.

Stag Hunt: A game theory example of safety and social cooperation. A group of hunters must individually choose: All must act cooperatively to kill a deer, which they can all eat or act individually where each one can kill one rabbit, which only he/she can eat.

Stalking Horse: The low-end bid on assets in a public auction. The auction company will select an entity (the stalking horse) from the pool of bidders to prearrange the first bid setting a reservation or floor price for the asset being auctioned.

Tug Boating: The need to slowly guide the other side to see the benefit of your position and ultimately agreeing to a contentious term in the contract. For example, "That term will need a tugboat."

Unanimity Rule: Formal voting process whose outcome requires all parties to agree on a specific issue. Very difficult to make progress or achieve the result. This rule is desired by the smaller entities in a multiparty negotiation as protection and risk aversion. Should be avoided as all costs.

Vendor Agreement: A contract detailing all the operational details and commitments of a retailer and its supplier.

Wal-Mart Quicksand: When you are being negotiated down over time at a slow and methodical pace.

Winners Curse: Nagging conviction the winner paid too much or did not get enough in the deal after the agreement is completed.

ZOPA: Zone of possible agreements. The range of acceptable outcomes between two parties bracketed by each other's *walk-away* boundary or reservation price. It is also known as a contracted zone.

Bibliography

"Negotiations." 2003. *Harvard Business Essentials*. Harvard Business School Publishing.

Bazerman, M.H. and M.A. Neale. 1992. *Negotiating Rationally*. A division of Simon & Schuster, NY: Free Press.

Brodow, E. 2006. *Negotiation Boot Camp*. Doubleday Publishing.

Carnegie, D. 1936. *How to Win Friends and Influence People*. A division of Simon & Schuster, New York, NY: Gallery Books.

Cathcart, J. 2002. *Relationship Selling*. CA: Cathcart Institute Lake Sherwood.

Gallagher, B. 2018. *How to Turn Down Three Billion Dollars*. St. Martin's Press.

Hartley, G. and M. Karinch. 2005. *How to Spot a Liar*. NJ: Career Press Franklin Lakes.

Hudson, D. and G. Lucas. 2010. *One Minute Negotiator*. San Francisco, CA: Berret-Koehler Publishing.

Stewart, J.B. 2005. *The Disney Wars*. Simon & Schuster.

Ulin, J.C. 2010. *The Business of Media Distribution*. Focal Press.

Wasserstein, B. 1998. *Big Deal*. Warner Books.

About the Author

Mike Saksa's 30-year career involved many types of negotiations working for Fortune 500 companies. He was able to survive, adapt, and thrive as a stakeholder witnessing crisis management negotiations in three well-known catastrophic business disruptions: Tylenol poisonings/product recall; the KKR acquisition of RJR Nabisco, which became the Emmy-winning movie, *Barbarians at the Gate*; and the AOL Time Warner merger, known as the worst business deal in U.S. history. In addition to his BS in Finance, MBA in Marketing, and MFA in Cinematic Arts, he received advanced executive training in Leadership and Negotiations at the University of Pennsylvania Wharton School of Business and Harvard University Graduate Business School. As a senior executive at Warner Bros. and Redbox, he led content negotiations against top retailers, professional sports leagues, streaming platforms, TV cable networks, movie studios, and celebrities, where he acquired, sold, and licensed over a billion dollars of content. He is a guest lecturer on entertainment industry disruption at the UCLA Anderson Graduate Business School and a USC Cinematic Arts Graduate School thesis panelist. This book provides a how-to-negotiate by establishing the negotiation edge using his strategies of compete, collaborate, and compromise plus lessons learned from 25 of his best and worst negotiation experiences.

Index

OTHER TITLES IN THE HUMAN RESOURCE MANAGEMENT AND ORGANIZATIONAL BEHAVIOR COLLECTION

Michael J. Provitera and Michael Edmondson, Editors

- *Forging Dynasty Businesses* by Chuck Violand
- *How the Harvard Business School Changed the Way We View Organizations* by Jay W. Lorsch
- *Managing Millennials* by Jacqueline Cripps
- *Personal Effectiveness* by Lucia Strazzeri
- *Catalyzing Transformation* by Sandra Waddock
- *Critical Leadership and Management Tools for Contemporary Organizations* by Tony Miller
- *Leading From the Top* by Dennis M. Powell
- *Warp Speed Habits* by Marco Neves
- *I Don't Understand* by Buki Mosaku
- *Nurturing Equanimity* by Michael Edmondson
- *Speaking Up at Work* by Ryan E. Smerek
- *Living a Leadership Lifestyle* by Ross Emerson
- *Business Foresight* by Tony Grundy
- *Negotiating With Agility* by Kathy Beyerchen
- *11 Secrets of Nonprofit Excellence* by Kathleen Stauffer
- *The Nonprofit Imagineers* by Ben Vorspan

Concise and Applied Business Books

The Collection listed above is one of 30 business subject collections that Business Expert Press has grown to make BEP a premiere publisher of print and digital books. Our concise and applied books are for...

- Professionals and Practitioners
- Faculty who adopt our books for courses
- Librarians who know that BEP's Digital Libraries are a unique way to offer students ebooks to download, not restricted with any digital rights management
- Executive Training Course Leaders
- Business Seminar Organizers

Business Expert Press books are for anyone who needs to dig deeper on business ideas, goals, and solutions to everyday problems. Whether one print book, one ebook, or buying a digital library of 110 ebooks, we remain the affordable and smart way to be business smart. For more information, please visit www.businessexpertpress.com, or contact sales@businessexpertpress.com.